STREET ENTREPRENEURS

A GUIDE TO SUCCESSFULLY GROW YOUR OWN BUSINESS, REBRAND YOUR IMAGE AND ACHIEVE YOUR GOALS

CHRIS NWOGU

STREET ENTREPRENEURS
A Guide to Successfully Grow Your Own Business, Rebrand Your Image and Achieve Your Goals
Copyright © 2021 by: Chris Nwogu

ISBN: 9798675978557

Published in Nigeria by: Emotion Press

My Centre gives way, my rights recede,
The situation is excellent, I shall attack!
-General Foch

Pay attention because you have never been this way before!
-Joshua

To
Jidechi, Tonna, Chizzy
A father loves too much.

StreetEntrepreneurs* is a must read for anyone who wants sure, simplified and precise ways to navigate the murky waters of success in building a business or career.

I have read quite a number of great books on entrepreneurship, sales and marketing but in *StreetEntrepreneurs*, Chris got all the answers and workable solutions wrapped in one single book.

It has managed to surpass my high expectations as a *"Double Plus Good"*.

Adaku Osondu-Ojomo
CEO, AdabelleBeautyNigeria

"A reliable entrepreneurship craft for all business startups and thriving businesses- it is practical, streetwise and Innovative
Idongesit Inyangabasi
Chief Executive Officer
Hewelt Systems Ltd

In loving memory of my first tutor, mentor, teacher and lecturer, who first held the bicycle until I could pedal. Patiently, held the chalk, pencil and pen till I could compose and scribble my thoughts. You laughed passionately and inspiringly as my crayon scrawled its first painting. You sat joyfully and graciously on bare floor that I could seat, crawl and walk – My mother, Mrs Justinah Nwogu. A mother's love is indescribable. Thank you!

Foreword

In his new book, 'Street Entrepreneurs', Chris lays out the immense challenges millennials and new generation of youths face in gaining a foothold in any economy especially in this post covid-19 era.

This debut compilation of information proffer solution-based strategies for any business or career to excel exponentially, sustain growth in perpetuity and climb effortlessly to the zenith in any given industry.

The tone and style of 'Street Entrepreneurs' makes it an easy read because it is inspired by strategic researches, confirmed business logic and empirical experiences of powerful iconic individuals, who have succeeded, phenomenally, in various treacherous terrains by modest means using new age best business practices, making their climb to the peak seem effortless.

Chris has outdone himself, once again, in his bid to help others achieve their goals, realize their dreams and reach their full potentials by expounding on these lessons, while revealing more efficient ways to make plans work beyond expectations.

This book brings hope to the challenged as it addresses major issues relating to unemployment solutions and introduction of innovations towards knowledge driven entrepreneurship.

I don't think there is anyone who wouldn't benefit from reading this '5 star book master plan'.

Engr. Dr. Mohammed Jibrin FAEng, FNSE, FNICE, FPA, FIMC
Director General/CEO
National Board for Technology Incubation

CONTENTS

PART TWO
LITTLE THINGS THAT MATTER- BUILDING PERSONAL CAPACITY

PART THREE
EYES ON THE PRICE! IT'S ALL ABOUT YOU.

DISCLAIMER
Names used in the stories and illustrations in this book are fabricated and does not relate to any organization or individual living or dead, any similarity is mere coincidence

All efforts were made to ensure the accuracy and reliability of information contained herein. However where human limitation or mechanical factors lead to omission, error, inadequate or incomplete information, the author regrets it and sincerely apologize for such outcome.

PREFACE

Chance favors the mind that is prepared
-Pasteur

During the cause of my job, especially after several speaking engagements, I've often been approached by people who had taken a long time, sometimes running into months or years, trying to figure out how to do things better, proficiently and professionally. They need answers to set up or reinvent a business, regain lost opportunities, kick-start or rekindle a dwindling career. This is a book of entrepreneurship, that brings solutions to the above questions and help you find purpose.

On entrepreneurship, below is an adaptation from an update from Immanuel Ibe-Anyanwu's social media handle: it brings to fore, challenges faced by new business

"The night that birthed the idea, the months it took to raise money, the internal debates about colour logo, theme and marketing strategy. The daily hustle to just tell the market that you matter –no one sees all these.

At the end, the audience may see only the late delivery and that's fine. People have their own problems and are not necessarily here to help you. They expect you to do it right.

If you are on social media, you will get initial support when you launch. But it's just friends and family. After that, the figures will so crash, you'll spend months, even years, to stand –if at all. It is the market telling you to do your own growing, that goodwill isn't enough.

You're going to beg influencers, media organizations, even your market for attention that will not come. It is not that they are bad people. The world is designed to identify mostly with success, so you will face contempt from circles you hoped to count on. It is what it is.

And here's the hardest part, you will most likely fail. Most enterprises fail in two years. Your ideas may be an illusion at the end, and you'll realize this only after years have gone by and you have nothing left. Workers don't like startups too, so lots of your staff will use your office time and equipment to get jobs elsewhere, so you're essentially on your own to put good mechanism in place to get it right as an entrepreneur.

For those wishing to dive in, much of what you heard about starting your own business is crap. The true lessons are on the streets and you need a formidable plan and strategy to win at the end.

However, only a few things can compare to that feeling of overcoming the odds, looking back at an idea that came in traffic, inside toilet, late night while lying on your bed or out of anger –looking back and seeing that idea now fully formed.

That feeling of having created something from nothing, something that is touching distant lives and enriching your own, of being an entrepreneur, rendering services, and creating job.

All human beings should have that feeling once in their lives –it is a feeling of triumph."

Street Entrepreneurs, is written as a guide to prevent you from going through a bleak and miserable experience as an entrepreneur. The above situation is common but it doesn't need to be. Business doesn't need to be that risky, uncertain and thankless, and you can get it right by starting right.

For the purpose of this writing, Street Entrepreneurs includes startups, existing small business, those in businesses of sales, manufacturing, merchandise, services, or hybrid business. They need better innovational and techno-digital knowledge to help them succeed and avoid mistakes. It includes formal and informal structure that identifies businesses that excite their interests and cash in the midst of challenges. Street entrepreneurs take their chances to create something of value intended to be beneficial for themselves and the society.

This book brings such information that will proffer solutions to these and similar problems help avoid reckless failure and guide you to reach your heights.

We do not need to be economical with the fact that we all are sitting on the time bomb of joblessness and global rise in youth restiveness as a result of unemployment for our young graduates. The danger that stares us in the face if we fail to find solutions is unimaginable.

It is inappropriate to think that government alone can cater for the employment needs of its citizens. We do not need further surveys to understand that government ministries, departments, agencies and other state-owned institutions are already over-staffed. Most of these staff are paid for doing less. There is need for those engaged under the employ of the government to prepare a forehand as most government employees may lose their jobs, with technological advancement in the work place. It is certain that more will lose their paid employment. These are realities that need to trigger national discourse and solution-based strategies, especially in the post Covid-19 era.

Across Africa, with an existing mass of unemployed youths, a recent study added that about 60% of 10 million students graduating from Africa's 669 universities yearly are not able to find jobs five years after graduation. This book aims to trigger entrepreneurship revival, reinvention, skill acquisition and vocational tutelage, in addition to formal education, as a means to assuage the crises of unemployment.

Recent studies show that as at June 2018, all three tiers of government in Nigeria accounted for a mere 8.4% of national aggregate demand. It means that the private sector currently accounts for a massive 91.46% of aggregate demand. This infers that government must work to meet the needs of the private sector. For, in the private sector, through startups, SME's and Street Entrepreneurs (Streetpreneurs), lies the strategy for self-empowered masses.

There is need to emphasize entrepreneurship, but not in the way it is often emphasized . Text books, tutors and, recently, Masters Classes, seem to lay emphasis on business being more about risk taking. I propose that this is not entirely correct.

The Igbos of eastern Nigeria are known to be very enterprising and to excel in any enterprise they channel their energies into. This pattern of good enterprise replicates itself wherever they find themselves across the globe, and this brings us to the big question which I have discovered the answer to: What drives them?

The Igbos rarely see business or entrepreneurship as risk taking, as emphasized in some business schools, entrepreneurship hubs and skill acquisition centers. They embrace it as one embraces and cares for a lover –with tenderness, attention and care, not entirely risk! Isn't love risky? But how often is love equated to risk taking? Who actually thinks of risks when embarking on a love affair, despite the reported strings of heartbreaks?

To the Igbos, business means seed planting, meeting needs, competition, empowerment, responsibility, goal, vision, dream, attainment, striving to consolidate and overtake.When you prepare your land properly, your seeds will germinate. When it germinates, you nurture them to the extent you can guarantee a good harvest. Occasional natural disasters and other circumstantial occurrences apart, no farmer considers planting a risk. Hence no one goes into a competition with a mindset of risk. You go to give someone a run for his money. Therefore, you prepare adequately. That is why Igbos spends years to train and prepare for their chosen interests of entrepreneurship properly. Risks must be in congruence with mastery of business knowledge; none should take precedence over the other.

The innovative modules presented in this book are gleaned from strategic researches and empirical experiences from both simple and urbane individuals who succeeded in very difficult terrains by modest means. The aim is to help others achieve their goals, realize their dreams and reach their full potentials by expounding on these lessons, while revealing more efficient ways to make plans work as expected.

Here is a book born of practical experience and current realities. It began after repeated identifiable occurrences of incidents which I did not go in search of, but was compelled to pay attention to. Consistent events formed threads of similar patterns, and ordinary people did extraordinary things in ways that should have required professional skills, great learning or specialized trainings. But these individuals made great accomplishments in the process.

Some of these people were educated while others received only informal training. Several acquired theirs from the streets, raw skills based on their hobbies or interests, and many excelled in their chosen vocations because they believed in their dreams and made painstaking efforts to make such ideas come alive.

This book came to be while taking a personal interest in processes that led to such huge accomplishments. I struggled to make connections with the kind of audacity that stirred bicycle repairers and printers to end up building the first airplane. The Wright brothers achieved such an accomplishment at a time when successful engineers could not have imagined such a feat. While I was rummaging in my mind about accomplishments by ordinary individuals, Channels Television (a renowned television station in Nigeria) aired the story of a young man at Oghara, a town in Delta State, Nigeria, who, without any formal training, made an airplane that stayed airborne and took aerial pictures of his surroundings. He had also produced his own aviation fuel to test his prototype.I came to the understanding that the baseline is the magnitude of dreams and the will to follow through. Such accomplishment pitches its root in dreams. Your dreams, audacious dreams, will always conceive ideas. Ideas have to be consistently worked on and boldly put in motion in a chain of activities that eventually draw and deliver success.

Again, I reasoned about the strength of conviction that spurred Obama, a son of a black immigrant to aim for the position of President of the most prosperous economy in the world and achieve such a great ambition in this era. I was also overwhelmed by the strength of personal belief that stirred Innocent Chukwuma of Innoson Vehicle Manufacturing, a man with no fantastic education and a 'barely enough' financial background, to conceive the idea of the first black owned vehicle manufacturing company in a country with unimaginable infrastructural challenges and in a continent where such was unheard of. Everything starts with the individual. It is all about you. It is one thing to dream, it is another thing to believe in your dream and have the discipline to prune, hone and work to make it happen over time.

Here is the fact; Streetpreneurs were not geniuses in their chosen careers and professions at inception. They were ordinary people who believed so much in their ideas. They worked hard on those ideas and achieved extraordinary results that inadvertently bestowed on them a class of genius and entrepreneurial distinction! Today their accomplishments have continued to encourage and inspire millions of people within and around the globe. All these could be attributed to a resolve to succeed. A resolve born out of bold believe in one's latent potentials and acquired skills, and turn obstacles into potent opportunities and tangible realities.

Of the men and women who excelled against odds, we may want to ask, what gave them the motivation and courage to stick to their ideas, believing they would work even when others thought otherwise? On a closer observation, their actions were as a result of shrewd confidence in their ideas, attention to details and 'can do spirit'. At other times, it was as a result of detailed thought-out plans of action, practiced over time, often in the solitude of their environment. That which seems spontaneous, swift and easy was actually groomed by the discipline of lengthy time-honored practices.Yet it could also be an inherent skill of raw genius nurtured into excellence. Of course we all have that shooting-star-moment of spontaneous insight, when great ideas flash and are captured in moments of plain inspiration-spasm of stray ideas caught at instants. Ideas that create possibilities, and enlightening and brightening aspirations. Regrettably, some of these out-of-the-box insights are often left to drift away untapped.

Street Entrepreneurs is a book that is aimed at motivating, instigating and provoking you to take action that breeds proactive changes, changes that lead to an empowered and fulfilled life. It's all about you and your dreams, ordinary dreams that produce extraordinary ideas. Ideas that are worked upon and put in motion in a chain of activities that eventually deliver fantastic achievements, bringing about a world of successful men and women. These chains of activities are the subject lessons of this book.

The book is divided into four parts:
Part one, WHAT'S IN YOUR HEAD: INSIGHT AND SELF UNDERSTANDING, covers Chapters   1 – 9 and deals with your insight and personal understanding in the pursuit of your dreams.
Part two, LITTLE THINGS THAT MATTER: BUILDING SUCCESS CAPACITY THROUGH SKILLL ACQUISITION AND PERSONAL DEVELOPMENT, covers the four chapters 10 through 13. These chapters capture developing and acquiring necessary skills that will help you achieve your goals. Following through this part will help eliminate challenges usually encountered in pursuit of aspirations.
 Part three is tagged EYES ON THE PRICE – IT'S ALL ABOUT YOU, and covers seven chapters, 14 – 20. The book concludes with the fourth part with chapters 21 - 22   tagged 'NEED WE REST ON OUR OARS?

In writing this four-part book, I bring to fore close to two decades of real-time, hands-on experience and practical knowledge. My persuasion to undertake this voyage stems from a bleeding heart, from constantly seeing numerous men and women make and continue to make similar or related kinds of mistakes. Often, they make wrong decisions that, despite their protracted painstaking efforts to plant and grow their dreams, ensure failure. Had they been equipped with the right information they would have succeeded. It hurts to see or hear of occupation, enterprise, careers or projects that have no reason to fail crash due to avoidable circumstances. The convergence of reasons that leads to this failure includes insufficient knowledge, plain ignorance, fear of making mistakes, outright impatience and a lack of will to proceed. This book aims at forestalling such situations from arising and provides leeway to mitigate them where they have already occurred.

In *Street Entrepreneurs*, I used practical true-life stories and experiences to buttress points and bring the work closer to the reader. I have strong optimism that you will be steered and persuaded to confront your fears and reach the heights of your aspiration. It is hoped that you will be persuaded to pursue that business or career in spite of the time you think you may have lost; to train and retrain when necessary and be bold enough to launch yourself to that dream that has kept you restless for so long.

My intention is that you may never be found wanting when your opportunity arrives and your opportunities must come because you have instigated them! Herein lies my reason and as such the qualification for writing, to bring this knowledge to public domain. It is my desire that as you go through this book, you may find its pages engaging, insightful, rewarding and tailored to your specific need. Kindly let me know if and how this book has been of help to you by dropping a line at **info@streetentrepreneurs.com.ng.**

LET'S GET ACQUAINTED

One man with an idea in his head is in danger of being considered a mad man. Two men with the same idea in common may be foolish, but can hardly be mad...
                    -William Morris.

When all are seating, faces glitter but when they are up and moving, you witness different shades of movements. So the question arises, will it be preferable to be idle with shinning faces or to navigate the uncertain adventurous journey of self-discovery and fulfillment? Come to think of it, despite huge discoveries made and still being made in medicine, engineering, artificial intelligence (AI), communication and virtual reality technologies and many other mind blowing inventions, many inventions are still born out of curiosity.

It is generally acknowledged that curiosity kills the cat. Curiosity can be likened to necessity which is known to rarely understand laws and generally agreed and accepted as the mother of all inventions. The tourist, traveler or the curious young lad who tours, associates and learns from people from different economies, different cultures, traditions, languages and literatures is more knowledgeable than the grey haired old man who acquired his wisdom in a particular locality, This is because travels broaden the mind.

For ages, men have known that information is power. Equipped with the right information, you are sure to do great exploits. In today's world of the internet, globalization compels us to acquire new skills to meet the volume of rapid information and technological know-how. This becomes necessary to meet the ever changing and fast paced markets! Of course, we are certain of the fact that there are ways that make end results more predictable. In your hands is a tool that will empower you to be more productive in your chosen endeavor. As such, we join Maya Angelou who penned these inspiring and beautiful words "you did then what you knew, and when you knew better, you did better". Yes, your success can be predictable just by your actions or inactions. This book seeks to inspire you to take those actions that guarantee success.

In my career journey, I have worked in research departments, account departments, stock department, marketing and sales department of various organizations across two decades. At one time, I worked actively to meet the demands and expectations in the field, and at other times, I worked in the dark suited cozy air conditioned blue chip offices. I later became an entrepreneur for the major part of this period. These journeys afforded me great privileges to be engaged in different positions, roles and field experiences comprising social, community, business circles, ideological think-tank, religious associations, professional gatherings and stake holders meetings, podcasts, virtual summits and conferences. This is also supported by my network of friends and acquaintances who were themselves entrepreneurs, employees, managers, directors of establishments and corporations, businessmen and women, inventors, scholars, religious leaders, civil society groups, traders, artisans, medical professionals, and even casual acquaintances in transit and everyday people.
The knowledge gathered from these associations led to further research that presented truths difficult to ignore, that you can succeed against all odds if you are determined and focused and you can begin again and succeed even after a disaster like the Covid-19 epidemic. Yes, tasks that have proven impossible even by experts can be successfully accomplished if you are convinced of that great idea and bold enough to believe you can make it happen.
Regrettably, this journey has also often thrown me off balance, bewildered when I see seemingly bright people with bright ideas that failed.
You can actually make mind boggling discoveries and inventions. You can also start those dream businesses or careers and you can live those dreams.

Consider Commander Robert Edwin Peary, reputed to be one of the first men to have reached the North Pole, after a difficult but successful trip, he penned these words:

"The grim guardians of earth's remotest spot will accept no man as guest until he has been tried and tested by the severest ordeal,"

Consider also, various minerals, pearls and other precious metals hidden deep underneath the earth, covered by layers of rock, located at the heart of mountains, sheltered at the bottom of the ocean, wrapped with shells, buried at sea beds or even bound somewhere above the atmosphere. You cannot just get at them. You must be up to your teeth to strike gold or diamond, and you must know exactly the area of its location as you conduct extensive exploration.

For when you know what you are looking for, you will know where you are headed, and only then will you choose the right route. Again, if you know your destination and the importance of your trip, no obstacle can be so extraordinary to dissuade you from your goal. An important mission will mean an abhorrence of delays and distractions. To accomplish your set task you must not only trust your tools but you must believe in yourself, your insight, in your training and sometimes, your gut feeling or intuition. This book promises to awaken all these parts of your personality and more.

The times we live in call more for the ability to adjust to changes as an entrepreneur and as a skilled professional. These are the lessons drilled from the global pandemic that caged the entire human race to their homes for almost half of 2020. I believe these experiences have unleashed the best in us to survive, to win and to seek better ways of providing sustainable income for ourselves, our families and society going forward. This is the book that will provide the needed guidance that generates successful careers, businesses and help us rediscover ourselves.

The eagle hashed among chicks and ducks is intuitively aware of a deafening urge to soar and ascend far into the horizon, but believing and knowing will not be good enough. It must keep attempting until it takes its place far into the skies and gazes directly into the sun even if everyone had told it that it was practically impossible to reach such heights. This is to say that you must know when to choose to go deaf to the honest opinions of 'chicken and duck' experts, and listen only to your heart to achieve great success. Only then will you begin a journey of street entrepreneurs, unleashing the entrepreneur within you.

Chris Nwogu

PART 1
INSIGHT AND SELF-UNDERSTANDING

WHAT ARE YOU DOING HERE?
Amadi works with the security outfit that guards the building complex where our firm was located. He was always neatly dressed, reflecting a confidence that's rare with junior staff. Committed to his job, he was diligent, friendly and polite. On a particular evening, after I had closed for the day, I walked towards my car, carrying some documents. Amadi had just finished doing his final rounds (inspection of the premises). He offered to help carry some of my documents to the car. Within that brief encounter as we walked towards my car, he had politely enlisted my help to look out for job opportunities for him. I smiled at his cleverness. When I asked what was wrong with where he works presently, his response was thrilling and engaging, "Ah sir, this job is just a means to an end."

"But you seem to enjoy what you do." I quipped.

"No sir, it's not passion, just that while it lasts, you give it your best shots as you wait for a better job somewhere."

"So what can you do?" He was a little hesitant so I asked him what his qualifications were.

"I have a secondary school certificate."

"How were your results?" I asked further.

"Excellent sir."

"Do you have any other skill?"

"Apart from the skill I have acquired as a guard I have no other skill but I don't really want to do security job anymore."

"Oh...but what skills have you acquired as a guard?

"The one you see me doing Sir, or is it not a skill?" He smiled in his jovial manner.

"How long have you been working this job, you mentioned that it was a means to an end?"

"Seven years, sir."

"And within that period, you've not thought of improving yourself for better advantage?"

"Sir, the job doesn't give much time for any other activity and it pays so little."

"No job 'gives that much time' you create time or you squeeze it out of your tight schedule. By the way, don't you work shift?"

"Yes, I work shift but apart from time factors, I have much responsibilities and obligations from my parents and five siblings. I'm the first among my siblings; the demand is so much that I can't even save or plan much."

"Oh yeah?" I interrupted.

"Sir?" he asked confused.

"It all fits," I responded. "The job doesn't give you enough time to do anything much, yet the pay is little. In addition, you have many other dependents and so you can't plan much with your income. You don't have enough to pay for further training yet you cannot meet your personal needs or that of your dependents and everyone including you keeps walking in circles, leaving you worse off."

"Well" he stammered, "that as well summarized it all sir, but can you assist me by looking out for a job that can help meet all this obligations."

"You need a job that will meet all obligations?" I stressed.

Amadi seems to understand what I implied as he stared in apprehension.

"Well, you will have to open a business but unfortunately even if you do, at the earlier stage; it won't give all the time and meets all your financial needs." I smiled to put him at ease. "But before then you have to create time and make sacrifices for self-development. You know your smiles and jovial nature alone will not put food on the table, unless you are considering taking up stand-up comedian. Although you can start this venture among your support group, or get training incustomer relations".

He was silent, so I continued.

"The job you do now if you plan well can give you enough time to develop yourself especially if you plan your shift. Let's talk next time." I said finally.

"Ok sir"

Settling into the driver's seat of my car, I turned to him and said, "Think about what we've discussed and see if you can come up with solutions of your own on areas you can improve yourself, acquire skills, further training, educational upgrade or even open your own business." With that, I drove off.

I ended up stuck in traffic for over two hours.An annoying occurrence, especially as my home was only thirty minutes from work. But there was a grid lock resulting from the road diversion orchestrated by the construction work going on that road. I was tired but I used that opportunity to run through my mind the discussion with Amadi.

Victory, triumph, or failure can result from approaches to life vicissitudes, issues, and opportunities. You are the product of your decisions. Whether you know or lack information and suffer the consequence, ignorance is not an excuse for how unfair life turns out. You must deal with the results of your approaches and decisions whether you take necessary actions or out of ignorance you were unable to do so. Take Amadi, for example, he expects a better life. Though ambitious, intelligent, and full of vigor, he has not devised better means to instigate such a change in fortune.

Expectations must be met and balanced with prudent planning, followed by workable time, program, personal training, and development. It is only then you place yourself in a position to attract and meet opportunities. In these times, a secondary or high school certificate alone brings more limitations in terms of job opportunities. Yet, it provides you fundamental opportunity and platform for further studies and provides leeway to acquire more skills or vocation that empowers you in the process.

Amadi's love for his parents and siblings is seen in his commitment to them, against his comfort. Still, he is neither doing them nor himself any good by his approach. Amadi's first need is self-investment and personal empowerment. Since his parents and siblings are not on an emergency condition, Amadi, distributing his meager monthly income, an income that could not meet these various needs, shows reckless financial intelligence, poor judgment, and misplaced priority.

He has only succeeded in being unproductive to himself or anyone, for that matter, even when he thinks he has been there for his family. While one may see him as a good son and caring brother, yet after all is said and done, Amadi is uninformed and, as such, lacks a strategy for personal growth. Good people like Amadi will most likely end up perpetually lacking and persistently in need of basic life necessities due to bad choices.

The Amadis of our time need mentorship and perhaps professional counseling. They need to read good books, attend personal development programs, and associate with a network of informed people who will assist them with quality advice and suggestions to explore and exploit their potentials. He needs to make disciplined financial sacrifice and adjustments for personal empowerment as a matter of urgency. Amadi needs either more educational qualifications or a skill to be better positioned and disposed to support his dependents and society.

Due to work demands and commitments, I never had time to discuss with Amadi for almost a month. When we later met, I immediately observed that Amadi must have had time to think about our discussion. He had come up with various plans and ideas. For the first time, he realized that his job could provide enough time and opportunity to run a two year part-time program in a tertiary institution. He was in his second year in the program when I was transferred to another state. Amadi later changed his job to another security outfit. We lost contact and never met again for a long time. I assumed he finished and perhaps may have gone ahead to get a higher diploma or possibly be in another job or even started a new business.

Eight years later, I ran into Amadi at a bank one evening when I came to withdraw cash via ATM. To my dismay, Amadi was still in security clothes, still doing the job he wanted so much to quit. Amadi was already wearing the feature of one that has grudgingly accepted life's hardships. I saw an Amadi that has lost the vibrancy, confidence, and ambitions of earlier years. Though I was happy seeing him, I couldn't help speaking out in disappointment, **what are you doing here?**

Amadi had changed to a better paying job, a job he knew might not give him time to complete his program at the polytechnic. But the appeal of more money blinded him from rational decisions. He had thought that since he was about to complete his two-year program, he could somehow maneuver to write his final exams. When the time came to write his final exam, his new organization told him to forfeit the exam for his job. Amadi made a choice that led to his decision to forfeit about two years of academic commitment. He just walked away from his educational pursuit to secure a job that never lasted two years. He traded his education for immediate financial gratification, another poor judgment, and misplaced priority. He had consulted with his friends and colleagues before deciding to forgo his two-year educational investment, a decision he has come to regret, but also shows the quality and group of people on his network. Again the relationships and association one keeps may be part of the reasons one has little or no advancement. It could also be part of the reason you may have moved far ahead in your endeavors.

I don't know where you are now. But by the time you had finished reading this book, I will love to see you practically navigating towards your aspirations. And perhaps if the question 'what are you doing here?' comes up, it will either be a result of a phenomenal growth on your part, that even with challenges and setback, you were intentional and never allowed yourself to be boxed into stagnation.

Chapter 1

NECESSITY BASED ENTREPRENEURS

The best time to plant a tree is twenty years ago,

The second best time is now

African proverb

We all have our stories -of captured moments, opportunities gained and lost, of decisions that turned things for good, mistakes based on youthful exuberances, failed dreams, loss of golden opportunities, lost hopes and aspirations, and many more. The journey of life is not always smooth, often we do not know the turn and curve life takes at those critical stages in our lives, but we can choose to turn things around, straighten or flatten the curve after each storm of life. It is called adaptability! The information you're about to get in this book is tested. It worked for me, my friends, and my clients. I assure you, it will undoubtedly work for you no matter where you're coming from.

Starting over again

I arrived home that day in 2004, and it dawned on me that I had no job! After putting about three years on the job, made sacrifices, traveled on emergencies at odd hours, and helped deliver sales and close deals that produced tons of sales for the company, I was devastated as I sat in my room alone, scared, lost in thought without really thinking. I looked at the household items, designer clothing, electronic gadgets, and leather seats I had acquired in these years. They seemed so useless. They didn't even have second-hand value to start with. None could solve my need for a job, nothing to fall back on, and my savings were fast dwindling and depleting.

I had started this job immediately after graduation, about four months on entering the job market. It turned out to be a special kind of job. It often involved traveling – my salient hobby, and there was money to be made. So in months that followed, I had already rented and furnished a nice small apartment in the Federal Capital Territory.

Barely a year later, I was already making inquiries on the type of car to buy. My major concern back then was a car with power, speed, and class. I later purchased a BMW 3 series. Then I began a relationship with my pretty girlfriend. We went shopping often, traveled on weekends, occasionally vacationed, road trips, sightseeing, and picnic. Life was good.

As at that time, most of my friends were still unemployed, so my house became a stopover for almost all former schoolmates who knew friends and me and were searching for a job. Some came for interviews and exams in Nigeria's capital city of Abuja. Others came over to ease the boredom and frustrations of unemployment. My immediate family, siblings, and relatives also came to visit sometimes.

All I did back then was spending money on expenses, purchasing household items, designer wears and providing for the ever constant visitors to my house. It often crossed my mind to invest in something; real estate, stock, bond was hot then, yet I kept procrastinating.

Overnight, things turned on its head. Crisis followed in chains! The job was gone, and every other thing followed in a thread-like pattern: the car, my savings, my friends, and relatives. Reality set in. I was broke and jobless! I had thought it wouldn't be that difficult to get another job, considering the contacts I believed I had built over the years. But as the weeks rolled into months heading to a year, fear and loss of confidence started to set in. I knew I had to something quickly. No, I can't continue searching for a job; not after all those papers I delivered as an undergraduate, during youth programs and as working-class in 'managing small-medium enterprises'.

It was time to walk the talk. I will admit that a combination of fear and survival led me to find a solution. Late night is always my time to brainstorm. For a week, I locked myself indoors thinking, sketching, running ideas, then it clicked. It was still more like a gamble. But I had to do something as I was convinced that searching for a job was not an option. My sketches, plans, and ideas were wired toward small businesses.

A week later, I had gone to the Corporate Affairs Commission (CAC) to register a business name, as that was the registration I could afford. That done, the excitement of registering my first company, a marketing firm, gave the feeling of one with a vision. Then I went to the printers, got myself a business card, designed a catalog based on the experiences I have gathered over the years from my previous job. I also printed introduction letters. After this, I made calls and emails to manufacturers, importers of similar products, competitors, and friendly clients and customers I had ever worked with.

Something was going for me; I had a good rapport with most of the people I dealt with while working with my former company. Some agreed to give goods on trust while others demanded little financial deposit, which I could not afford at that point in time. With that, I set out to market my new company, and a new business was born.

The first six months was the most difficult of my entire life, but six months down the line, about a year later, in 2005, I had posted sales of over $85,000 and had in my employment two staff.

One thing is sure, the lockdown orchestrated by the Covid-19 pandemic, though regrettable, provided the world an unprecedented opportunity for review. The world was on a form of control experiment with the chance to gaze into the past and peep into the future from a present where communities, states, provinces, regions, countries, and continents were locked down for close to 5 months!

Many were forced to think outside the box, recalibrate and reset their ways of thinking, pursue careers, and do business. It also opened the mind to adjust to changes and not be taken unawares, and be financially prepared for future occurrences. The lessons learned during this lockdown are numerous.

It's a known secret that sustainability through salary and savings has been overrated overtime. Money saved and nicely tucked away into banks safe is mere degraded money unless wisely invested.

Many one-source income homes barely lasted a month after years and decades of salaried work and savings. Most were looking for government palliative not only to augment their savings but also to survive the lockdown. Before our very eyes, unemployment surged, company and organizations shut down as the entire globe grapples for survival first.

The experience of the lockdown has got people thinking about entrepreneurship and alternative source of income. This global pandemic will change the course of doing business the world over. If we're deliberate, we shall come out of the pandemic steered by a renewed entrepreneurial spirit, equipped with new convictions, new knowledge, and skills to make the best out of the future for us all.

Not long ago, a picture went viral on social media; it was of black men of African descent selling roasted corn on the streets of Europe. While this could be a little disheartening, it also struck a chord in my thought of businesses carried out on the street, homes, car packs, etcetera, to survive the moment. It was an emergence of necessity-based entrepreneurs. From some of these unpopular places will be unleashed street entrepreneurs who will eventually turn their fortunes around if they are deliberate and make the needed sacrifice and commitment.

While it may be irrational for anyone to travel overseas or anywhere just to roast corn in the streets, it is a possibility that these guys may have been short-changed by the pandemic lockdown and are trying to survive at all costs legitimately.

One can argue that most are not planning to stay in that business more than necessary. They may be selling roasted corn to overcome the needs of the moment, but the street can inspire the emergence of new businesses.

It has been noted that the post-Covid-19 era will bring about lots of necessity-based businesses and investments, SMEs, startups, and small and mega entrepreneurs. However, as much as this is expected, therein lies the danger.

The urgency will mean little or no prerequisite knowledge or skill to sustain and succeed in the business. Many of these businesses may eventually pack up due to inadequate knowledge, skills, and right personality needed to thrive as an entrepreneur.

To forestall this from happening and provide that bridge needed to be the best in your domain is the lessons delivered here. It will help you create your own successful dream business, career, and personality, even when you come from a very rough background.

Chapter 2

FROM STREET ENTREPRENEURS TO CORPORATE BRANDS

We wouldn't ask why the rose that grew from concrete has
damaged petals. Instead we would celebrate its tenacity; we would
love its will to reach the sun

–Tupac Shakur

In chapter one, we discussed necessity-based entrepreneurs. This chapter would deal briefly with transforming from street businesses to corporate brands with an eye on innovation. Many big brands started from the street and strategically positioned to what we see today and admire. Apple, Amazon, Google, and even Disney were said to have started from Garages!

While I can say with a level of certainty that Street Entrepreneurs or Streetpreneurs are the way forward to help rebuild the economy through local businesses in the post-covid-19 economy. These new businesses must have the knowledge and skills for later transitions from street to innovative corporate positioning.

New entrants have ample mentors to glean from the street and learn how they could get their street businesses started from unlikely places to become global brands. Innocent Chukwum of Innoson Motors, Cosmos Maduka of Coscharis, Dangote Of Dangote group, and many others were once Street Entrepreneurs.

Recently Sijibomi Ogundele, one of the youngest Nigerian billionaires, in 5 years and at age 39, built his luxury real estate company worth over $400M, the Sujimoto Group. Sujimoto builds extraordinary edifice in premium neighborhoods of Ikoyi and Banana Island, with annual revenues of approximately $30M. It all started at Oke-Arin Market and later as a souvenir hawker in France[1].

Richard Branson of Virgin had an early stint in publishing' Student magazine'. He later went into recording as virgin records label and eventually Virgin Atlantic Airlines. Today, Richard Branson controls over 400 companies with a net worth of over $4.5bilion.

The story of Samsung is one such that made a shift from a Grocery store to various businesses until the Giant Samsung electronics brand was known and admired across the globe today. It all started on the streets.

We are officially global citizens, a generation with a full grasp of technology through digital platforms with linked data sources bringing about unimaginable innovations. This era is where knowledge has come to be equated with digital skills that add value to new business and existing industries. Streetpreneurs must seek to leverage technology for a truly functional and successful business and entrepreneurship venture. It is estimated that by 2025 machines and robots would have cleaned out a substantial amount of jobs globally. The entrepreneurship landscape is fast changing as a result of the covid-19 pandemic.

Businesses across the globe are shutting down. Statistics show that about 70% of the workforce employed by SMEs were dropped across the world during this pandemic. The highlight is a society littered with skilled, unskilled, and highly skilled job seekers. Some of these individuals know the challenges of searching, applying for jobs, and getting jobs is slim in these times.

They include highly skilled employees in various fields, including high tech facilities with superior technological knowledge and tools. The good news is that some of these highly skilled individuals who lost their paid employment will embrace entrepreneurship. The great revelation is that these skilled individuals will think out of the box when they embrace entrepreneurship.

---

[1] Source: nairametrics.com

The loss of jobs is expected to create a new set of entrepreneurs from the streets. Also, they are highly skilled and innovation-minded considering where they are coming from. Expectedly, the loss of job from the pandemic will bring about necessity-based entrepreneurs and innovation-based entrepreneurs. The good news is that most will also be coming in with lots of innovations. In addition to these sets are those that will embrace entrepreneurship as survival strategy. They will contribute to reinventing the economy. New businesses are already sprouting in leaps and bounds to meet the needs of the times orchestrated by the pandemic. Some of them are already well established.

Facemask, nose shield businesses have been unleashed and are in high demand. This becomes necessary, especially as governments legislate on citizens' compulsory use of these preventive measures.

Small factories are opening up, and other existing SMEs are reinventing their business to take advantage of the moment's needs. Food business has embraced innovation as deliveries are becoming the new normal instead of people coming to restaurants and breakfast houses. E-Businesses, digital marketing, e-commerce business, network marketing, and multilevel marketing are becoming the new normal. Data is the new juice, and information business has finally been linked as the world's new currency.

For job seekers, the choice going forward will be determined by entrepreneurship's direction and ability to add values, especially through digital skills. Today's job seekers will be people that will be able to create value through skills that meet the needs of the time. Acquiring new skills and new knowledge that fits traditional education will bring about proficiency in the workplace.

There are lots of uncertainties, waiting for these new businesses. Many new entrants, even when starting with enough tools and innovations, will be lacking in knowledge. Good knowledge of business and skill to manage the business will ordinarily guarantee success as entrepreneurs and businesses. Lack of basic knowledge will lead to failed businesses. In all, those who lose their jobs will be disorganized and disillusioned; many may become down and out.

A few years ago, it dawned on me that entrepreneurship is the way to go if we are to extricate our society from the burden of unemployment and stimulate the economy to productivity. The pandemic provided a challenging terrain to do business, depending on where one views from. When one focuses on the challenges, he/she will see only difficulties and an inability to make progress.

Elon Musk is a brilliant mind who created start-ups that became incredibly successful, like Tesla and SpaceX. Elon is said to know nothing much about rockets when he came up with the idea of SpaceX. It was too ambitious and risky, a project that few entrepreneurs would venture into when you consider the high stake risk involved. But by reading lots of books, Elon built up his knowledge and skill.

To achieve this, Elon Musk incorporated identified experts in rockets across the globe. Going into Rocket business was a big risk that could lead to huge failure, but Elon is a risk-taker[2]: "failure is an option, if things are not failing, you are not innovative enough." Today both Tesla and SpaceX are huge success stories leading and changing the scope of technology and bringing about new world revolutionary innovations.

The Tolaram group is a common example I find absorbing: how to proceed and invest in difficult business terrain and tough times. Tolaram understudied the situation and developed winning innovative business models that set the trend of noddles business in Nigeria. They turn around things and make the noodles business an admired venture that has attracted other business followers in that industry.

---

[2] Sylvian Saurel

In 1998, Nigeria was not the premier investment destination. Life expectancy was 46 years, gross domestic product (GDP) was about $23 billion. GDP per capita was about $256, 78% of people lived on less than $2 per day; about 37% of people had access to sanitation, while 58% had access to improved water source. Nigeria had experienced six coups in its 28 years of existence as a republic. It was under military rule in 1988, and in 1998, Nigerians happily welcomed General Sani Abacha, a military dictator. This wasn't the best time to invest in a country.

But Tolaram paid little or no attention to those statistics when they saw the noodles business's quantum of opportunities. Their only thought was of how to overcome it and mine 'the gold'. Tolaram started importing instant noddles into Nigeria. Since then, the company has integrated into the country and grown its Indomie Instant Noodles sales to a staggering $700 million a year. In the process, the company is selling more than 4.5 billion packets of noodles each year. Today Tolaram has over 17 manufacturing plants in Nigeria (including Noodles, flour, Palm oil, Seasoning, etcetera), a packaging company, and a logistics company with over 2000 trucks[3]. Today Indomie has become a staple food in Nigeria, grossing almost $1bilion in revenue.

Fixing the basics

There is a need for street entrepreneurs to go back and learn the basics, even when they have succeeded in their chosen businesses. This will be crucial for sustainable success. If they fail to understand these basics, it may come to haunt them someday, having noted that some of these new entrants might succeed naturally due to the skills they go into business with. Where instant success occurs, they may relegate the need to go back and learn business basics. Failure to fix the gaps may let loose a high price to pay in the future. An example of relegating the basics happened in the boxing ring recently, at the MGM Grand Garden Arena in Las Vegas, Nevada. Saturday 22th February 2020, the fight

[3] Source: Efosa Ojomo Dec, 15, 2015 Medium .com

between Fury and Deontay provided a classic example of the need always to strive to fix the basics. It also exposes the cost of ignoring such and the price paid in the day glory beckons. Although Deontay maintains that Fury defeated him because of the elaborate outfit he wore on his ring walk that weighed 40 pounds, many argue that the defeat resulted from the failure to learn the basics.

The fight between these boxing greats was one boxing lovers across the globe anticipated. These enigmatic and iconoclastic personalities were to have a take on each other. On one side of the ring was Tyson Fury, the Gypsy King, and the other side of the ring was Deontay Leshun Wilder, known as the Bronze Bomber. Tyson Fury came into the ring with prefight records of remarkable scores of 29 fights with 29 wins, of which 20 were by knockouts (KO) and a draw. Deontay Wilder went into the ring with prefight records on 42 fights with 41 wins. Were 41 were on knockouts and a draw. Deontay was the first American boxer to hold held the WBC heavyweight title for 9years (2015-2020)

Both boxers came into the ring with an incredible resume of unbelievable fights records with staggering wins that fuels a champion's mentality. The world of boxing was looking forward to knowing who among these boxing greats was a better fighter.The argument was settled on the 7th round. Tyson Fury won the fight on a technical knockout, becoming the world heavyweight champion with a new record of 30 wins and 21 knockouts (KOs).

According to boxing pundit, Tyson Fury may have won because, based on some boxing analysts, Deontay refused to fix the basics he missed during his early career journey. They argued that sudden and instant success has its adverse effects. Having tried very various vocations ranging from truck driving to football, Deontay discovered that he was a natural fighter in his early 20s. He probably believed that his dangerous right hands, which guaranteed that he kept winning and knocking out opponents, could make up for the basics. When he was told to learn these basics, he thought there was no need for it.

Tyson, who had studied most of Deontay fights, at that night of glory, capitalized on those basics Deontay refused to learn. It was a night of blood as Deontay bled from ear, nose to the extent that his side had to throw in the towel in the seventh round. Foundations are fundamental.

As the post-covid-19 era brings about new entrants to the business, many will succeed immediately. However, they will need to learn the foundation and basics of their chosen trade and acquire new skills and knowledge to make tremendous and sustainable success.

Chapter 3

WHEN DREAM WAKES YOUR BUSINESS INSTINCT

It does not do to dwell on dreams
And forget to live
- J.K Rowling

How often has that idea, plan, or dream kept you awake for the best part of the night as you keep going through the picture over and over in your mind's eye? How often have you awakened from a restless sleep because the thought of a particular idea could not let you sleep peacefully? How often have you found yourself staring at the horizon, entertaining your mind through the power of your dreams, and imagining things as if they were already existing?

Dreams feed our curiosity, speed up our creativity, stimulate our intellect, and inspire great ideas. Nobody is so skilled, gifted, or talented that he/she does not spend quality time going through his dreams and ideas before setting it up.

Often, our dream jolts us up from our aimlessness and indifference, causing us to take actions, risks and eventually draw people to us—people who believe in our plans with a corresponding drive to pursue and facilitate the achievement of our goals. Your dream can wake you and cause you to take action. This can happen when you have the inner motivation to pursue it.

Idleness is akin to death; it leads to retrogression. Idleness comes due to a lack of dreams. Dreams cause you to search deeper and help stimulate ideas. Stray ideas can be trapped, especially when we filter such ideas and pick them apart. This process leads to action. However, it is not all action that leads to progress. Only purpose-driven action will accelerate progress. Progress is like a track event aimed at finishing the race. The difference is that you are not all competing for the same trophy. Here, individuals move at their own pace. The tracks are measured and marked equally.

Given effort and focus, all will arrive at their destination but in their own record time. You are placed in your track by a design and technique you are familiar with and comfortable with. If you focus on that track and work hard, you will eventually reach the finish line. Arrival doesn't have to be the same time as others. All that is needed is focus, consistency, and making haste slowly without distractions.

We typically exact so much force, so much energy when we want to reach the same time, often leading to a collision. When you leave your lane and enter another's, you would have not only disrupted and cheated on the other person but also yourself. Even if you win, you will pay the price, the penalty of which may disqualify you, expel you, or make your effort futile and more demanding. This means that you must focus on areas you can easily express yourself, your skill, or your interest in life. These are your areas of strength. It is in these strength areas that you can always find motivation. As a race, it starts with a dream, seeing the finishing line in your mind.

The man who continually dreams without working to bring it to reality in practical terms is locked up in mere daydreaming. He is like the proverbial drunk who explained that people erroneously think he is crazy because when he wants to say a particular word, another word jumps out of his mouth. It is a dream when you make an effort to make it count.

Dreams can be your wake up call to take action. Take charge of your life and live that life you've imagined. But first, you must dream, and if, like most humans, you love to be held in high esteem by your friends, colleagues, families, and your contemporaries. It is time to dream, and this time, you must dream big. It is in your dreams that ideas on how to achieve them are dropped, captured, and used to create realities.

Always create time to brainstorm. Ideas can drop in at different times and circumstances. These ideas must be written down or sketched on paper or other devices of your choice. Such saved documents may lead to problem-solving, more creativity, and stray discoveries someday. All thanks to that which you had written down and perhaps never knew how valuable they are at that point in time.

Even if you do not want to immediately use the idea, always keep them secure where you can retrieve them when needed. Someday you will be amazed when you go through ideas written down at the spur of when your brain is active and occupied with an idea that has kept you restless. Late-night relaxation on your bed or favorite sofa could provide quiet, uninterrupted moments to meditate and work out the future you will like to chart your course while also reflecting on the past.

Of course, inspirations, insights, and ideas can drop in at varying places, moments, or situations. However, quiet moments and meditations will afford you concentration that results in productive ideas. It is in that quiet time that you traverse the core of your imagination, bringing to life your dream in ways you would never have thought possible.

Running one's own business is a dream many would love to come through in their lifetime. It takes will power and personal conviction to decide to be self-employed or run a start-up. Running a business needs a passionate commitment and constant motivation. It can be interesting and rewarding in the long run.

Ours is a society on the rise. We must leverage this and take advantage of the numerous opportunities available to us. Young people are often energetic, promising with great zeal to do things. This zeal should set the stage for the new group of young entrepreneurs who will usher in a new generation of empowered, vision-driven, farsighted change agents. Amid numerous problems and teething challenges lies our unique vast sea of opportunities. When we find ways of solving these problems and meeting needs, a business is borne.

There are hundreds of software applications needed in our environment that are yet to be created to solve our problems, meet our needs, and reinvent our economy. Applications to tackle the menace of corruption, electoral manipulation, and fraud, wrong census figure, contract award, transport business to monitor drivers, educational software to monitor school system, programs, and teachers performance the lists can be endless.

Of course, I am aware that it is not all of us that will have individual businesses. Some will not even dare think of it because they believe they lack what it takes, lack great ideas, and the decisiveness entrepreneurs are known for. Others are better when they are told what to do by their boss. The latter individual is better as a paid 9 am - 5 pm employee.

In a small house fellowship I attended a few years back. During the prayer section of the program, one of the members said that his employer, the Federal government, was about to start retrenchment in the ministry where he works. According to him, those affected will be handsomely rewarded. The amount is such that they can even start a capital intensive business with the severance benefits if they chose to run their own business.

He said he would not be able to start a business, talk more of managing one, as he has been a civil servant all his life. He mentioned that he does not even know what to do and how to go about it. He went on to say that he prefers his monthly salary. Although it was not much, it was regular, and he was better off with it. He wished that such downsizing, no matter the amount of compensation paid, should not affect him. He prayed to retire when he was due and then stay home and enjoy his pension!

Many people are like him, and not being a business owner does not make them lesser persons. Such people will also contribute to the growth of businesses and organizations in other important ways. Identify them and allow them to help steer your business to a greater height. Such individuals must find their purpose and follow it diligently. No one knows you as much as you know your capabilities. The danger is that when the first challenge comes, you get blown away because you lack the resilience and fortitude that entrepreneurs are known for. Of course, we know that sometimes our fears are wrongly magnified, and we fail even to dare to try due to the fear of failure.

Reasons people go into business

People start a business for different reasons, but the underlying reason is to make a profit. Some start a business because they are tired of taking orders and instruction from others. They loved being independent and innovative. They love taking independent action and make decisions of their own.

Others aim at helping humanity by creating employment for as many unemployed as they can. They also make a profit in the process. In contrast, others start to give back to society in the form of aids, foundation, and other philanthropic work from profits made. Some start their own business to have money to live freely and pursue hobbies, take care of their families, loved ones, relatives, friends, sponsor religious programs, and finance developmental projects.

Some go into their own business to have a chain of businesses and conglomerate, which gives them a sense of fulfillment, power, and authority.

Businesses have also started bringing innovation to existing ones to turn such a business line around for good. Yet few others run a business out of greed and to run others down. A business will make you wealthy, and such wealth will gain you favors and increase your status. It brings your friends, good medical care, and attention. It will also give you some form of protection and happiness.

The Three Footstool of Success

Before you let your ideas fly, you should consider what I regard as the three footstools of success. Playing down on any of this gives you a stool a foot short. These are:

· Passion
· Motivation
· Building relationships

Passion

"Nothing great," says Georg Wilhelm Friedrich, "has ever been accomplished in the World without passion."

It is that passion that will keep you going when the chips are down. Take a football player, for example, he enjoys playing the beautiful game and is paid for doing what he enjoys. This means he never gets bored with it. Even before he had gone professional, rarely a day would pass without training and practice. Take him to a new environment. The same day, he would identify the neighborhood team. Within days, he would have joined them playing; this he does because football is his passion.

Ask yourself, how long can I last with this business? Can I do it for two years, five years, or will I be bored out in six months? Passion breeds motivation, passion, and motivation will keep you going even at your lowest time. In all this, nothing much will be achieved without setting a time frame to accomplish your goal or project. Without setting a time frame, a project that will otherwise take a year could take five years. Having a set time for your project prompts you to work more. Timing helps you strategize and go straight to your targets while remaining focused on your designated task. It prevents you from getting distracted.

FIND MOTIVATION

In business, constant motivation is required even if you have an excellent product or super skill. Routine can be boring, wiping out creativity. Challenges and uncertainties are inevitable and could be demanding, tasking, discouraging, and unpredictable. Finding motivation keeps you going. Conceive or find out what motivates you.

Students or undergraduates may be motivated by a better future to study more. Excellence and success can be your motivation. Fear of failure could motivate you to succeed. Poverty can be a source of motivation to succeed. Fear of a poor old age can steer one to think out of the box. Health challenges can also motivate you to make health discoveries. Perhaps it is said your race, ethnicity, or religion does not succeed in a particular field; proving such negative belief wrong could be your motivation. Providing your spouse, children, entire family with the best that life could offer could be your motivation. Just as looking at the faces of poverty-stricken children and poor masses could be the motivation you need.

With motivation, the fire that spurs you will keep burning. You must improve on what you have, where you are, and what you do to stay relevant.

BUILD RELATIONSHIP WITH YOUR CUSTOMERS

A successful business seeks to build a relationship with its customers. Such a relationship should be at its highest quality of customer service. Customer relationship continues in and out of the business premises to how the business is perceived outside. The quality of customer service influences a good perception. In today's business environment, 'over-the-top services' (OTTS) have come to describe the highest quality of customer service.

All businesses aim to make profits. In doing this, meeting the needs of customers becomes paramount. There should be a deliberate strategy to improve customer relationships. A loyal customer is far more important than your immediate profit twice multiplied. This is because a loyal customer will stick to your product and attract some of their friends, colleagues, and relatives to it. This, in turn, becomes a network of loyal customers. What profit could be more than this? Don't just sell your product, market relationship. Relationships are the life of every business.

Today, Return on Relationship (ROR) has been added to the business lexicon. ROR refers to the loyalty and recommendations that can arise from nurturing relationships. Old relationships alone can keep your business on a breakeven level, but it cannot sustain future commitments. This means that you must treat your old customers like kings, your new ones like queens, while you treat your expected clientele as princes. All are royals and deserve the royal treatment.

Successful marketing involves enriching your social capital at the base and identifying and taking advantage of the trend in your business line. A trend is not static; it keeps changing over time. A business needs to adapt and move with the trends, or it goes obsolete. Being obsolete or outdated stems from a lack of creativity and an inability to introduce new ways to improve quality. Lack of innovation can transit to poor sales and, by extension, financial loss or, worse, business closure.

Take advantage of the internet to market your product, set up your company's website, and learn to market online. Your product, marketing, and staff attitude will reflect the success or failure of the business. Ensure excellent product quality, prompt delivery of goods or services, and attention to your customers' needs.

These customers are the reason you are in business. Meeting the needs of a client should be paramount to your success. Wealth is a product of conditions met, and customer relationship is the Holy Grail of business success.

Your product must do what you say it does!

To capture their share of the market, new products often time are released to consumers as top quality products, especially those products and services with an existing competitive brand. There are observations where some businesses come up with products that endear the market to them. When they see they have captured the market, they gradually reduce quality to maximize profit. This is customer deception, a betrayal of trust bestowed on them by their customers.

This action may bring temporary gain. It is only a matter of time before the knowledge of such deception gets round, especially in this information era. Nothing causes business failure as a reaction from disappointed clients. Any business operating on this premise will eventually collapse; it's only a matter of time. Business integrity is essential. Integrity remains the key to attracting and sustaining the market share of the business. Integrity keeps products active in the market.

Lack of integrity can destroy a business faster than any other factor. In the long run, customers will eventually find out and can no longer trust the product; words go round, and the damage may not be remedied. Integrity forms the core value of great organizations, a pledge to maintain quality.

Great organizations are those who maintain quality. They understand the importance of their customers' relationship and trust, and they do not take it for granted. In trying times or when price increase becomes necessary, they do that, bearing in mind the increased burden on their customers' pocket. When market forces and cost of production compelled them to adjust and increase prices, they make an increase in price to reduce the burden on their consumers. This is the reason they retain customer trust over the years yet keep going strong in marketing.

Have you ever wondered why of all beverages in the market, you always go for a particular brand or product? Of all electronic gadgets and automobiles, it is only a particular company's product you enjoy over the years. Sometimes when you try to switch to a new brand, you still return to that previous company's products. This could be because you've tested, tried, and have come to trust the brand, and it gave the same satisfaction and experience it promises to offer. Remember, your product must do what you say it does.

Chapter 4

IMAGINE-A-NATION

No problem can withstand
The assault of
Sustained thinking
-Voltaire

What image can you build in your mind, products you can create, or inventions you can develop? What is the nation you would like to have through your imagination, the life you will like to live, and what you will want to accomplish? Just imagine it, and from that wild fantasy, your nation could be on the way to being built.

It all depends on what that nation is to you, yet it all begins with your imagination's depth and richness. For when great idea meets imagination, you imagine a Nation; perhaps the reason imagination could be open up to IMAGINE-A-NATION! Spread your imagination and soak yourself into it; therein begins your power to build your nation.

The Wright brothers mentioned earlier were bicycle repairers. Yet, they dared to believe they could build an airplane that could stay airborne. They didn't just imagine it; they believed in what seemed like a crazy outlandish idea. This was at a point in time when others thought such a feat was practically impossible. They saw the end from the beginning by imagining it possible, and eventually, they made their lofty dream happen!

When you soak yourself in your idea, you live it, and you see it in your mind's eye from where you stand. Imagination allows you to see things from perspective and direction that others wouldn't have thought possible.

One Saturday morning, I gave a lift to a teenager in my neighborhood. As we drove through a street to cut off heavy traffic, we observed a group of men, residents in the area on voluntary community service. They were repairing their street drainage system and raising a short concrete wall to stop pedestrians from using a particular path. As we drove by, the young lady riding shotgun mentioned casually that these men would cause flooding with what they are erecting. The observation was so plain and casual that I did not even pay attention to what she said.

Days later, I drove through the same street; heavy rain had left the neighborhood flooded. The flood entered some houses, and I saw the same group of men with chisels, hammers, and diggers breaking down the wall they had erected about a week back! It was then I recalled the casual comment by that young lady.

A job that took a group of men hours to do took a smart teenager less than ten seconds to casually point to the effort's futility. Numbers might mean power in a democracy, but numbers do not always proffer creativity or solutions in the fundamentals of progressive action.

Of these few who excel against the odds, we often ask what gives them the drive and courage to stick to their ideas, believing it will work even when others think otherwise? The answer lies in their imagination's richness, a firm conviction that transforms this imagination into ideas, and an effort that propels it to reality.

Below are examples of a few persons who were dedicated to their ideas and conquered.

Kanu Nwankwo

Kanu, fondly called Papilo by friends, admirers, and colleagues, may be seen as a classic example of turning difficult and near impossible situations into great opportunities and accomplishments.

As a poor lad whose family could barely afford three square meals daily, football became a passion that absorbs and erases these lacks. He passionately played the game with other kids on the rough Street and uneven terrain of Owerri.

Kanu was often accompanied by deprivations occasioned by poverty. Unbeknownst to him then, Kanu was receiving his life training in a sport he will eventually be decorated above many of his contemporaries.

As a professional footballer in Europe with Ajax and Internazionale, Kanu established himself as a skilled player and cup winner before moving to Arsenal in the Premier League.

At Arsenal, he was later relegated to a substitution role. This position would have fitted the title of 'super-sub' due to the achievements he made from his sub roles. Here he once held the record of third most substituted player in Premier League history-making appearance from the bench in a substitute role in a record 118 times. Yet from this unpalatable substitute role, Kanu raised the bar. He rose to the occasion, an act that culminated in great accomplishments, glory, and prominence.

Kanu proved that it is not where you are placed that decides your fate, but what you do from where you are placed. Likewise, the most embarrassing failures can be turned into triumph. When he would have been demoralized, Kanu chose to create possibilities from that demoralizing sub position!

Soon after Kanu won the Olympic gold medal with his Nigerian teammates in 1996, Papilo was diagnosed with a heart defect leading to heart surgery in 1997 to replace his aortic valve. This close shave with death led to his establishing the Kanu heart foundation. This organization provides free heart treatments to children, especially African Children with heart defects.

Despite obstacles and setbacks, Kanu seems to always have a reason to keep moving, rising to a new peak after each challenge. He remains one of the most decorated footballers in the African. Kanu has in his kitties:

A UEFA Champions League Medal
UEFA Cup Medal
Premier League Winners Medal
3 FA Cup Winners Medal
Olympic Gold Medal
Two Times African Footballer of the Year Awards and hosts of other Awards and medals.
Kanu is also a UNICEF Ambassador.

In recognition of his exemplary beneficial services to youth across the globe and Nigeria, the Nigerian government conferred upon him a merit award Honours of Officer of the Order of the Niger (OON). Kanu has proven true the popular parlance that it is tough to defeat a man who never gives up.

General Muhammed Buhari

What could have spurred General Buhari, a former military head of state, that made him keep believing in his aspiration to lead a democratic Nigeria?

It may have been a tenacious belief and desire to bring sanity to corrupt Nigerian leadership. This tenacity is seen in his doggedness to lead the most populous black nation even after serially being defeated in three previous presidential elections.

He was labeled a serial failure, an unelectable, vindictive, military dictator, ethnic and Islamic bigot. But one thing went for him; both his admirers and detractors seemed to agree about his integrity and incorruptible posture, an attribute the voting masses from religious divides believe will be needed to cleanse a system reeking with gross corruption.

On his fourth attempt at the age of seventy-three, his opposition party All Peoples Congress (APC) defeated the ruling party People's Democratic Party (PDP) of the incumbent President Goodluck Ebele Jonathan!

General Buhari's dreams and aspirations were achieved in his fourth attempt making him the oldest Nigerian to take the mantle of the presidency. It was also etched in the record books for the first time in the country's history that an incumbent president was defeated in a general election!

All things are truly possible to the bold who exercise power to see the bigger picture despite rejections and failures.

Innocent Ifediaso Chukwuma (Chairman, Innoson Vehicle Manufacturing)

The emergence of Chief Innocent Chukwuma, Chairman of Innoson vehicle manufacturing Company (IVM), is a story of how discipline, boldness, hard work, and determined mind can break bounds and lead to unimaginable breakthroughs.

Innocent, youngest of 6 children, did not inherit wealth. Here is a man who had lived and educated to secondary level in his village in the highly commercial and industrial town of Nnewi, Anambra State Nigeria, known majorly for motorcycle and automotive spare parts.

That someone as Innocent with little education will eventually rise to become owner and Chair of the World's first black-owned manufacturer of commercial vehicles, utility vehicles, passenger cars, heavy-duty trucks, tires, and tubes is a testimony that life's deprivations and challenges cannot cage the bold.

Today his various business interests span not only vehicle manufacturing but also plastic products and household items.

His industry, Innoson plastic factory reputed to be the largest in Africa, produces over 150 different items, including machinery parts, motor parts, airplane parts, office equipment, household items, chairs, school desks, and various other items. His long walk to success started in 1978 after completing his secondary school education.

Innocent had wanted to study engineering in the university, but while waiting for his result, he kept busy in his older brothers' drug store. It was here he discovered his natural flair for trading. When the result was eventually out, Innocent did not meet the required grade for further education, but he had already made up his mind to venture into business.

In 1979, with the help of his older brother, who registered a company, Gabros international, trading in motorcycles, Innocent was given the sum of 3,000 Naira to start his new business and a free hand to run it. It was also from this initial capital that he rented a shop and bought merchandise.

By 1980, it was discovered that Gabros International Limited was making ten times more income under Innocent's guidance than the medicine store.

About two decades later, his establishment of two mega businesses, Innoson Tech and Industries, Enugu, and Innoson Vehicle Manufacturing Company (IVM), Nnewi, brought him to the limelight across Nigeria and Africa.

Innocent's goal is to produce quality but very affordable cars in the caliber of the Toyota corolla. He dreams of making imported second-hand vehicles unattractive to Nigerians by manufacturing attractive cars at affordable prices with available spare parts[4].

Colonel Sanders

If you like the taste of Kentucky Fried Chicken (KFC), you might wonder why Colonel Sander's idea was rejected 1009 times over a period of 2 years. Here is another typical case of boldness and tenacious belief in an idea. Only the bold can go through a thousand and nine rejections and not find an excuse to give up. Colonel Sanders rugged on, in firm resolve. He had already seen the bigger picture in his robust imagination as such, no

---

[4] www.naija.com/62600.html *(from spare parts trader to motor giant)* www.nairaland.com

disappointment, time lost, and embarrassing rejections could deter his conviction: "I made a resolve then that I was going to amount to something if I could. And no hours, nor amount of labor, nor amount of money would deter me from giving the best that there was in me[5]."

Looking closely at Sander's life, he indeed came across as a loser. At the age of 14, he dropped out of school and hit the road. He tried some odd jobs as a farmhand but hated it. At sixteen years, he lied about his age and joined the army but hated it too.

When his one-year service was up, he headed to Alabama and tried blacksmithing and failed. At age eighteen, he got married, and within months, his wife announced she was pregnant. On the same day, he told her he'd been fired again.

One day while he was job hunting, his young wife gave away all their belongings and returned to her parents, but he kept on while working at a succession of railroad jobs.

He tried studying law by correspondence but dropped out. Colonel Sanders also tried selling insurance, selling tire, running a service station but nothing for long.

Too soon, he was sixty-five years old. The years had slid by, a lifetime nearly gone and nothing to show for it. The United States Government sent his first pension cheque and told him he was old. But something inside him seems to explode, he took his first pension cheque of $105 and started a new business, and it clicked! He became the man who failed at everything except one. This business he started with his first pension cheque was Kentucky Fried Chicken[6]!

Yes, all things are truly possible to the bold who exercise power to see the bigger picture despite rejections and failures. The firm

---

[5] www.nairaland.com
[6] How to Survive In The 21st Century.Pg 72-73

conviction in their great ideas may have been anchored in the power of their imagination; they could see the nation they could call to birth despite the setback.

I refer to Imagination as the science and art of the mind to create possibilities. Imagination is a gift bestowed on every man to develop vast potentials. It sees the future as if it already exists by looking beyond the veil and manifesting great realities.

Our imagination could be as wide as the ocean and as deep as the sea. It has no boundaries, no rules or limitations, no ownership claim. Yet, it is a force that has propelled men to great achievements, greater than their wildest dreams and desires.

Imagination is unique to humans; a great mechanism that can lead to limitless possibilities and achievements. You can roam your mind with deep imagination as you please, farther beyond time and space.

Imagination can give one insight into their destination and the course their life will take. Unfortunately, many dismiss imagination as mere fantasy. To them, it becomes a mere daydream –that will never be called to reality. No great accomplishment has been made without first imagining it and working it to existence. Bold men imagine where they are going, what they need to get there, what it will take to get there, and how it will be when they get there. You can imagine a place you want to be, be there through your imaginative mind, feel it as if you are in that place.

Great houses and castles have been built through the power of imagination. Great discoveries and accomplishments have been made through imagination.

We can roam and visit places with the power of imagination. Great writers write of places they have never been and probably would never be. They write in ways you will be convinced that they are from such an environment. So do engineers, artists, men of innovative mind, creating, transforming imagination into ideas, and real-life masterpieces.

It all originates from their pipedreams from wildest imagination, a glimpse of ideas, stray thoughts trapped, toyed with, and brainstormed. Seeing the big picture in mind with conviction, that such a great idea is achievable.

Take William Shakespeare who on his posthumous birthday, Andrew Dickson of the BBC writes:

"Shakespeare in his lifetime may have lived between London and England yet wrote poems, sonnets and stories of worlds he never visited, a mind that roams free to "temples of lost civilization and onto dusty ancient battlefields, up to rampant Danish Castles and Scottish hills forts; across swaths of eastern Mediterranean and down through orient into Turkey and Egypt. He had a fascination of Italy, especially the glittering cosmopolitan city of Venice, minor obsession with islands (Cyprus, Sicily). His casts number Venetians, Viennese, Moroccans, ancient Romans, Ancient British, Ancient Trojans, Ancient Greeks… medieval Welsh, Irish, English soldiers, troupe of French Lords who dress up as Russians Muscovites."

Imagination knows no bounds

William Bourne, the 17th Century English Man whose basic design for the first submarine was amazingly close to our modern-day Ships, authored these words:

"And also it is possible to make a Ship or boat goe under the water unto the bottome and so come up again at your pleasure."

The idea of ocean vessels and the submarine, which though its basic design came from that 17th century Englishman, may have also had its origin as far back as ancient Greek when Archimedes discovered the Buoyancy principle: The force acting on or buoying a submerged or partially submerged object equals the weight of the liquid that the object displaces! During the later century after the William Bourne era, the building of experimental submarines was witnessed. Eventually, the submarine design took off during the 19th century and was adopted by several Navies.

The submarine was first used during the First World War (1914-1918). It was not long before the nuclear scientist started dreaming of a nuclear-powered sub, driven by Uranium Pile. Such dogged, ambitious dreams came to reality through the leadership, determination, and courage of men like Captain Hyman. G Rickover, which eventually saw the launching in 1954 of the US Nautilus.

By 1955, the World's first nuclear-powered ship went to sea, achieving the impossible by reaching the North pole 90 degrees north by 1958!

Today, the submarine features majorly in military usage, intelligence gathering, and reconnaissance missions. Civilian uses of the submarine include marine science, salvage, exploration, and maintenance. The sub can also be modified to perform specialized functions like search-and-rescue missions, undersea cable repair, tourism, and undersea archeology.

Credit should be given to William Bourne and those great thinkers of the distant past. They did not feel apprehensive about putting their imagination to public scrutiny. While many did not live to witness the actualization of their dreams, their ideas and basic designs became the foundation upon which modern accomplishments were made.

Today, many travel under seas and oceans by Nuclear Powered Submarine! This was a bizarre dream in its earlier time when it would have been a ridiculous, bold idea.While growing up, we watched James Bond perform lots of stunts born either from science fiction or Ian Flaming fantasies and imaginations. Earlier writers noted that the movies were futuristic, either preceding technological inventions or popularized conventional technology.

Of course, one can only agree that the techs were truly ahead of its time.

Below were some other futuristic technologies out then:
➢ Ejector seat
➢ Bullet Proof glass in Gold finger
➢ Mini binoculars in Living Daylights
➢ Voice Changer in Diamonds
➢ Underwater Camera in Thunder Balls
➢ Neptune submersible in Diamonds
➢ Killer Laser Satellite and gadgets
➢ Steel teethed Henchman
➢ Invincible weaponry cars that drive even in rivers while the Pager in 'From Russia With Love' filmed in the '60s, may have introduced the mobile phone we use today.

These were all born from the author's imaginative fantasies. Today, in reality, many of these science fiction (Sci-Fi) and fantasies are used even in the most remote areas. Our imagination can take us far beyond our time.
Napoleon Hill wrote, "First comes thought then organization of that thought into ideas, and plans then transformation of plans into reality the beginning as you will observe is imagination."

Imagination must be set into purpose-driven motion, propelled to action, or else, it ends up as mere daydreaming. It is like faith, something you strongly hope for and are so convinced that you can achieve even when you cannot physically see it at the moment. Yet, you visualize it as if it already exists. We can imagine- a-nation!

We are a product of our plans, imagination, and what we did with such sustained thinking. We are the outcome of our protracted inner thoughts.

People have been known to imagine for themselves what they want to be in the future. In later years through hard work, focus and resilience became that which they had conceived. This can be seen in every profession like acting, writing, music, football, medicine, law, engineering, art, science, and technology to merchandise, craft, and other vocations.

They all begin by imagining. In the bid to achieve their potentials, these men and women in such fields gave extra to earn these accolades.

They didn't just stop imagining it. They gave much more, perhaps the reason a Wiseman once told his audience that 'courage is failing over and over without losing enthusiasm.'

Thomas Edison put it succinctly "to invent you need a goal, imagination and a pile of junk" we must agree that he spoke from experience. Despite being a genius, he kept researching, trying many different ways until a breakthrough was made. Unfortunately, many have imagined great life that never came to fruition.

The 2003 hit song by Dido, "**Life For Rent,**" has its lyrics loaded with meanings:

Life For Rent:
I haven't found really a place that I call
Home
I never stick around quite long enough to
Make it
I apologies that once again I'm not in love…
It's just a thought, only a thought

But if my life is for rent and I don't learn to
Buy
Well, I deserve nothing more than I get
Cos nothing I have is truly mine

Here is where the song gets more interesting in context of imagination and sticking to plan…
I've always thought

That I would love to live by the sea
To travel the world alone
And live simply
I have no idea what's happened to that
Dream…
While my heart is shielded and I won't let it
Down
While I'm so afraid to fail so I won't
Even try
Well how can I say I'm truly alive

Reviewing the lyrics of that song, to transform imagination into reality, you need to learn to stick around for a while with your idea. Work hard and smart for its realization; else, you realize you never tried out those great ideas towards the end of your life. The implication is living the remaining days of your life tormented and apologizing for things you failed to do because you think you were shielding your life from the pains and embarrassment of failure.
In business and many areas of life, consistency, and continuity unleashes progress in the long run. Being known for a particular product could be more rewarding than being everywhere. Sometimes, being everywhere can mean no specialty, which is, being very good at nothing.

While you imagine that life you so desire, you must work towards it despite the piles of junk, mistakes, frustration, and mockery that comes up. Never lose sight and never be distracted from your goal. Relax and organize your thought, set your goals to keep working on them, and only then will you need no apologies for things you failed to do or things you did.

Albert Einstein declared that "the greatest power is the power of imagination." To him, that is the limitless stretch of one's imagination. "Imagination is more important than knowledge, for while knowledge defines all that we currently know and understand, imagination points to all we might yet discover and create."

Walt Disney, a nineteenth-century millionaire, coined an inspiring word 'Imagineering', combining imagination with engineering. Walt did not look for the Engineer who restricted his thinking to what his blue pencil and calculator said was possible. He looked for the person who dreamed big dreams and proceeded to make the dreams happen[7].Walt is known to be the transformer of the entertainment industry. He was known as one who possesses one of the most fertile and unique imaginations the world has ever known. To be better in his talent, he got educated further in his interest areas. While at McKinley High School in Chicago, Walt divided his attention to drawing and photography and attended the fine arts academy at night to better his skills.

It is not enough to dream, fantasize, imagine, or even have a vision and out of the box ideas. It does not matter how talented or gifted you are. Even natural talents can be honed to be at it its best. You need to put your foot down and take action. Seek to educate yourself more and learn as much as possible and assemble necessary tools to actualize dreams. The aim is to develop yourselves and make your imagination a reality. In their book, The Art Of Thinking, Allen Harrison and Robert Bramson wrote about an adult education teacher, Mary Ann's strength in getting her clients to ask themselves specific hard questions:

"Where exactly do I want to be a year or two from now?
What are my resources for getting there?
What specifically do I have to do in order to meet my objectives?"

You can live that life you have imagined if you prepare and put your imaginations to work.

---

[7] *James Walker: Husband Who Won't Lead And Wives Who Won't Follow*

Chapter 5

ACCOMPLISHING TASKS AGAINST ODDS - THE ZELOPHEHAD INSPIRATION

Better a victory achieved by wise counsel and dialogue
Than conquest won by fiercest instrument of war
-CON

To be successful, you must not necessarily be as strong as the lion. Still, you will have to be as fearless as the tiger in making decisions, taking well planned and thoughtful actions without falling into the danger of procrastination.

Fear has reduced men who would have been otherwise successful and great achievers into mediocre. Success in life demands that you be keen-eyed as the eagle to detect opportunities where the majority passed by. While you are at it, you ought to be as fast as the panther because delay has proven to breed regrets. There may likely be another smart guy in the arena that also sees the opportunity you are seeing.

Strive Masyiwa, founder and Executive Chairman of Econet wireless group, stated, "in every idea you have, there may be two or more others elsewhere working on same." So the faster you are to take your opportunities head-on, the better.

Reflect on your life. You might find a time you made very peculiar and daring bold decisions that seemed crazy to others but later paid off. Maybe it had to do with applying for that job you thought you had no chance of landing. You applied all the same, and to your surprise, you were invited for an interview, and to your amazement got the job.

How about those highly rated academic institutions you thought you wouldn't be offered admission into, yet you applied, and out of the blues comes your admission letter. Or that pet project or invention started in boredom that turned out to give you public attention. The great feeling of being ten feet taller by your triumph might have left you pleasantly breathless and overwhelmed with a sense of accomplishment.

What about the presentation before which you thought you would die of fright, perhaps due to the status of your audience. You got started all the same, and in a short while, you started getting approval nods from your audience. At the end of the presentation, as you step down from the podium, engulf by roaring applause and resounding cheers.

What of the office 'dullard' who eventually solve the problem 'intelligent Guys' were unable to solve to the amazement of all that won him approval from the hierarchy boosting his personality, confidence and forever changed his life for good.

Consider that proposal you submitted with other towering figures and giant of industries. Yet, yours was chosen ahead of other intimidating names!

Bold people do somethings that seem crazy and foolish to others. While unsung by colleagues, associates, community, and even relatives, they keep singing until they are heard.

Jack Canfield and Mark Victor Hensen - Over 140 publishers rejected their book "Chicken Soup for the Soul, yet the book, when eventually published, turned out to be a bestseller with over a million copies sold.

What drove them to ignore over a hundred and forty rejections, and stuck to their idea, an idea that they believed in, even when the experts and professionals in publishing firms thought otherwise and refused to publish their book. They had a strong belief and conviction in their great idea, with an imagination that saw beyond the present.

J.K. Rowling. The original Harry Potter and the Philosopher's Stone were said to have been rejected by a dozen publishers, including big publishing houses like Penguin and Harper Collins. Bloomsbury, a small London publisher, is said to have only taken it because the CEO's eight-year-old daughter begged her father to print the book.

Before she published the Harry Potter series, Rowling was in poverty, severely depressed, and a single parent. She became one of the world's richest women in only five years through hard work and perseverance.

Poverty, single parents, depending on welfare, and severely depressed -What recipe for failure could be more? What logical reason for failure than the above combinations? But not this bold woman that life's vicissitude could have left fragile but who in the face of daunting challenges cultivated an imagination as lively and fertile enough to ignore obstacles!

Constraints were turned into stepping stones because of an idea she wouldn't give up. She saw beyond what the experts were not seeing and refuse to let go. These women's story was the story of perseverance to a cause, as seen in the likes Innocent Chukwuma of Innoson motors, Kanu Nwankwo, and Colonel Sanders.

These were bold men and women whose great belief in their ideas won't just let them quit even when experts' opinions suggested they do so.

They kept singing until they were heard by those that matter to their plans, and once they were heard, nothing could stop the progress of a loaded determined mind.

The Zelophehad daughters

Another example of planning and getting a result against odds is that of the Zelophehad daughters[8] and their request in an era that was patriarchal when it was rare for women to speak publicly. As at that time, such a request was unheard of, against accepted societal norms and ethos. It was a weird request that would have resulted in their being stoned by the crowd of audience.

This was an era when the inheritance was based solely on male lineage. It has been, how it is, how it was, and how it will continue to be. It was the custom of the people, the religious statement and fiat ordained by the deity. This was a status-quo that could not be altered!

What the sisters did?

These five daughters of Zelophehad went to Moses, their leader, Eleazer, the high priest, the princes, and the entire congregation. They demanded their inheritance since their father had died without a male child and, as such, without lineage even though he had five daughters.

The sisters made a very convincing and compelling case to strengthen their demand to Moses and the entire leadership. Accepting this request would be going against the belief system and divine mandate. Yet mindful that it would be unfair if nothing was done about the appeal of these women.

Moses took their request directly to God, and God granted their request. This became the basis for sharing inheritance all over the land. The verdict states, "In the event there is no male heir, possession will be transferred to daughters, and if there are no daughters it will be passed on to brethren, if no brethren then to kinsmen."

Now you can imagine the attitude of the congregation when these bold ladies earlier made this request. Yet unwavering by such attitude, these ladies made a demand that positively changed their society, which altered the cause of history and forever improved

---

[8] **Numbers 27:1-11**

and liberated future generations of women. The Zelophehad daughters, by their convictions, improved their generation and future generations.

An interesting observation of this story may perhaps reveal how these five daughters (Mahlah, Noah, Hoglah, Milcah, and Tirzah) might have strategically positioned themselves as they presented their case. They were fully prepared, and when you are prepared, it means you have checked and tied every loose end and, as much as possible, bring it to your advantage.

Preparation brings to the fore your hidden talent, inspiration, and presence of mind to get it right. Imagine the five of them in various strategic positions where the people would be compelled to pay attention to them. It was as if the congregations were inclined to pay attention as these ladies pushed to their limit.

They may have positioned themselves where they could be heard and seen by all, no matter where seated, convincing the congregation by superior exposition and presentation.

Remember, these young ladies were five in number. They stood in strategic places as they presented their case to be heard by all dignitaries, decision-makers, and the entire congregation. Here are the five and possibly how they stood: Mahlah stood before Moses; Noah before Eleazer, the priest; Hoglah before the Princes; Milcah before all the congregations; and Tirzah by the door of the Tabernacle.

The congregation would most likely have seen these women's actions as arrogant. It was unusual for women to speak and address a crowd, especially during religious programs, ceremonies, or festivities. As if that was not enough, they continued, wasting no time presenting their case:

Our father died in the wilderness. (Fact is known to all)

And he was not in the company of them that gathered themselves together against the Lord in the company of Korah. (Verifiable, just in case you have forgotten or thought he was among)
Why should the name of our father be done away from among his family? (Moral burden, deal with it)
Because he had no son? (Rhetoric question, whatever answers you give, places a significant moral burden of partiality on you. Ignoring it means affirming what they are saying, so you have a weight of conscience to deal with).
And then comes the clincher, if what we just said to you is the truth, then, give unto us, therefore, a possession among the brethren of our fathers.

No wonder Moses hurried to a higher power for a solution. Boldness must involve a carefully thought out and articulated plan of action, as with these women. Boldness, as seen by the action of the Zelophehad daughters, results from well thought out plan of action, an action that visualizes the entire picture brings a positive result. It is a conquest won by a well-articulated plan of action, a victory accomplished by intelligence and wise counsel without resorting to palace intrigue or outright war for supremacy. Planning the Zelophehad way involves these core elements:

- Confidence in yourself and your idea
- Knowing the fact, having the fact and presenting an organized fact
- The humility of knowledge must stand tall above arrogance of knowledge
- Perfect timing is essential
- Courage to proceed against odds
- Detailed planning
- Thorough Organization of facts
- Concise and compelling exposition and presentation.

Neglect of any of the above core elements makes boldness nothing, but all noise with no bite, as Shakespeare expressed, "tales told by an idiot, full of sound and fury signifying nothing".

Napoleon once stated, "the art of war is a science in which nothing succeeds which has not been calculated and thought out." By the victories recorded in his military campaign, few will doubt the wisdom in these words. Of course, we acknowledge that war is a bold stance, aggression needing close to the perfect strategy before getting involved. Often, wars are won before they began because of the level of preparedness of the parties. The Zelophehad daughters averted crisis and, by extension, chaos by their well-planned presentation.

I remember when I went to a friend's Passing Out Parade (POP) at Nigeria Defense Academy. It was interesting to listen to stories about the rigorous training cadets go through during their years of training at the academy. That way, they were ready to take up any perceived threat in defense of their country. When necessary, they are trained to make the ultimate sacrifice of giving their lives. In a war situation, they may go beyond training received during their time in the academy, improvising survival strategies in the heat of battle or when isolated from their squad. Running a startup is close to the boldness of a military campaign. The business's success or failure will depend on the attention to detail, just as in a military campaign. This includes having a good plan of action, inventorying all you need to succeed, making sure you make necessary tools available, courage, and resilience, including your faith, which will also be tested during the process. You will need to marshal out your ability to be decisive even in dangerous and uncertain times when there may not be time to seek advice.

In our time, many have to take bold steps and actions that their contemporaries considered foolish. They ignored condemnation, let down, mockery, rejecting generally accepted 'wise' councils because they believed and are passionate in their ideas. Eventually, they made loud accomplishments. All things are truly possible to all that exercise their strength by believing and sticking to their great ideas. All these are achieved by timely and detailed planning.

Chapter 6
FRIGHTENED MEN

The impediment of action advances action,
What stands in the way becomes the way.
–Marcus Aurelius

We live at a time when fear has become a universal pandemic and often ill-fated derailment. Fear to love fiercely, intensely, and wholeheartedly. Fear to invest and fear not to fall to fraudulent hands. Fear of natural disasters. Fear to leave freely. Fear of uncertainties, fear of diseases in which the entire world was on a lock-down. The visual media, print media, and social sites have not made it any easier, as they are awash with daily scary news of terrible events.

An elderly couple, a very religious man of about 70 years, once received a prank letter from kidnappers. He and his wife were so frightened that he developed high blood pressure. This resulted in health conditions that they have been managing since the incident, even though the kidnappers never visited their home.

Armed robbers also attacked a house in an estate. Five blocks away from where the robbery took place, a woman was so frightened that she lost control of her bodily functions. She passed out urine and feces on her body while sweating profusely and struggling to breathe freely. She was later rushed to the hospital's emergency unit and admitted for days, even though the armed men never came to her home. These are some fatal responses triggered by fear. Fear is so destructive that peaceful cities and states could turn into war front overnight. People could move from states they have lived all their lives, places where they have built relationships, and made all their investments.

There are also real-time effects of fear in our society. Cities have developed systems of segregation where a particular religion or ethnicity is rejected in their home state and country. Neighbors who have lived together in peace and harmony look at each other with distrust and cast aspersion on themselves. Previously booming businesses fail, and well thought out business plans tailored to the nines are crash. Some now prefer to play it safe because of bad experiences or because of the experiences of others. So they decide not to venture into business. They fear to step out, try something new, invest their resources, and hold on to the niche that nothing is guaranteed.

Crowded by these occurrences, like a snail, many withdraw into shell and form cyst as their passion burns off. Better not to try than to try and fail is the consolation. The fearful mind convinces itself to wait until the next election, next government, next season. With this mindset, opportunities that stare in the face are left to drift away.

A lifetime has passed too soon, and they ask what happened as they now remember opportunities forgone. They watch in regret as their contemporaries, colleagues, neighbors, friends live comfortably and at times left behind a good inheritance for their kit and kin.

Painfully they recall that the same opportunity or decision that secured the future of others was also presented to them, but fear of failure hindered them from taking the necessary action.

The poet Charles kabuto Kabuye captured the above in his poem THE GREAT ESCAPE.

THE GREAT ESCAPE
We are frightened men
Men without core or guts
We move and act by group control;
We fear everything.
…we fear to declare.
Or discuss the movement of our humanity.
Inside us our passions work
Our emotions have ecstasies

And our sentiments see truth;
All visions for our common survival
But few of us will lift voice or finger to acknowledge or utilize.
We escape even the best flower
That fruit of our living flames of life.
Hiding in the twilight inches in escapism
We never grow up to required maturity
For our eyes of depth and width
Though active and sharp, never see,
Or face the light, the epiphany of life and meaning embodied
We so hide from ourselves,
Remaining unmapped oases to ourselves
And when we die
The utility of our body self
Faces that lie, the fear of our unexplored self
Once so rich in gifts of joy and discovery
Yet all left with all energy and riches untouched

From time immemorial, fear has locked in the minds of men. Fear
is a natural phenomenon wired into our structure for fright, flight,
and fight (3F). The 3F is a decision each of us will continue to
make in every circumstance at every chapter in our life as we deal
with situations. What we chose in each case will be seen in the
result generated.

Fear is a defense mechanism, a survival instinct for the continued
existence and preservation of man and animal. Man can use fear as
a tool for making good informed decisions. Fear can be creative
and motivating when properly channeled. Fear increases adrenaline
production, pumping chemical hormones and blood at a faster rate
to our body, especially our hands and legs for attack, defense, and
escape. It keeps us from harm. This is why we reduce our night
movement, where there is a greater chance of danger. Fear keeps
us alert.

When we are afraid, we will be inclined and duty-bound to be very articulate. We take a closer look at the situation that causes fear, thereby making more informed decisions and choices. By that, we pay more attention to our senses, which are needed for our survival and progress, eventually increasing our productivity and increased life expectancy.

Unfortunately, this is not always the case. To succeed in life, our fears are to be constantly kept in check. It should be conquered and kept in a healthy balance. Sometimes problems are magnified, blown out of proportion. They break down the body defenses and threaten to breakdown the individual. Fear can be extremely damaging and destructive when out of control. Fear slows progress, impair memory, snuff out prospective business life, and kills relationships, murder ideas. It provokes wrong decisions, loss of talent, skills, and lack of confidence.

Fear can be contagious. I have witnessed a whole market place shut down because one fearful individual misunderstood what he saw and started running. Others followed, thinking something dreadful was happening, and chaos ensued.

- Fear slows the wheel of progress
- It disintegrates plans
- Breeds denial of reality and brings about self-limitation
- Students, especially those who are not well-prepared, lose all they had studied in the exam hall due to fear.
- Children run away from homes due to fear of the consequences of negative actions they committed. The examples of fear-induced decisions are numberless.

Decisions made in fear often end in failure or fiasco. The journey began on a platform of fear that will sometimes meet with loads of obstacles. To be successful, you need more boldness and less fear to succeed. The fear factor needs to be addressed and objectively compartmentalized before vital decisions are made. To make decisions bothering on fear, the following questions should be taken into consideration to know the impact on health, business, social, and life impact:

- What is the source of fear, identify it?
- Why the fear? Is it real? If real, can it be minimized, eliminated, ignored, or turned to advantages?
- Are there consequences – how will it impact your overall outlook?
- Am I afraid of what people will say- public opinion?
- Am I afraid of gifting adversaries' talking point if I fail?
- Is it fear of failure or afraid of making mistakes?
- Is fear a result of poor or inadequate information?
- Do I need further research to overcome this particular fear? Do I need to consult with someone?
- Do you have someone you look up to? Can you think how he would have handled it?
- What will happen if you make or do not take that decision?
- What is the worst that can happen?

When we compartmentalize these issues, the solution begins to emerge. We often realize it is not as bad as we had thought. Sometimes the answers unleash newer and more vibrant perspectives that help us arrive at better solutions against making irrational decisions.

Another aspect of fear that leaves people at the foot of the ladder is the fear of failure. Often such persons are afraid of making mistakes. It is only when you make attempts and fail that you discover wherein lie your strength and weakness. This helps you learn better ways of handling similar situations in the future. It adds to your pool of experience and sharpens your intuition. This is in line with the words of Winston Churchill "Courage is moving from failure to failure without losing enthusiasm."

All human inventions and accomplishments originate from prototypes that failed or were unfinished at a point. There has been a failed and uncompleted experiment on the electric bulb before

Thomas Edison picked up and had the breakthrough with the incandescent bulb that could last longer.

Many works were done on an airplane before the Wright brothers built one that could stay airborne. As I sit writing, as easy as it can be with my laptop keyboard, scholars today, agree that earlier writings appeared pictorially in Iraq known then as Mesopotamia, and gradually substituted by complex system of characters. Later writing in inks using reed brushes and pens as seen in early Egypt hieroglyphic writing appeared from whence it continued till the manual typewriter took centre stage. Then the manual typewriter took centre stage. Today our computer keyboards have made writing easier. What if the previous experiments were discontinued out of fear of failure?

Uncontrolled fear can stop you from daring to attempt the simplest actions. Remember that all-time classic Rock band, Smokie, you could stay twenty-four years of opportunity "Living next door to Alice" without the will to approach her until she drifts away from your very nose.

Are you one of the people doing a job they do not enjoy? Do you lack job satisfaction yet spend many years in self-imposed distress because of the fear that another one may not be available? Sometimes you see people who keep knocking at a closed door that they unknowingly close their eyes to numerous opportunities surrounding and staring at them. Others have bright ideas but lack the will to realize it even when they can do it while holding their regular job.

Some time ago, two friends applied for a job and were invited for an aptitude test. On arrival at the venue, they noticed about a thousand other applicants invited for the same test. One of the ladies was so hit by the crowd of applicants for a job that required less than fifteen vacancies. She immediately packed her things and decided it was best to leave. Her friend and housemate tried in vain to persuade her to stay for the test. But she replied, "see the crowd,

I understand they are employing less than fifteen candidates from this crowd, I can't survive a hundred, and how can I get a chance in a thousand."

Two weeks later, the friend that did the aptitude test received a text message from the organization inviting her for documentation and training. She got a lucrative job. The difference between the two friends lies in their response to bad experiences. This is seen in their level of determination, confidence, self-worth, and ability to take ones chance at all-time even in the face of challenges and previous failures.

The other friend who left had a low personal drive to succeed; such people find reasons to quit on themselves. She lacked self-motivation and has been affected adversely by previous disappointments, which have created personal doubts. The consequence is seen in her low self-esteem. She fed fat on the fear threatening to tear her down even when that fear was unnecessary.

She did not take the exam even when she had nothing to lose by taking it, yet she went home to do nothing. She magnified her challenges beyond what they are. Referring to situations like this, Dr. Dwight. K. Nelson writes:

"It may be fear of defeat, a sense of failure that you are of less worth than others in your class or office or profession- 'who are obviously more successful than you' afraid to dare, afraid to try, afraid to ask…could it be that the fear of defeat has you on its clutches."

Granted, in our real world, multimillion-dollar businesses fail; the statistics do not help the lily-livered who are considering business. They have seen betrayals that strike in them fear, intimidations, natural disasters, assassinations, business failures, terrorism, and various forms of man's inhumanity to his fellow man.

News that was heard only from distant lands, countries, and continent now happen in neighborhoods. Businesses are crashing;

some experienced entrepreneurs trusted and believed to have Midas touch have seen investments fail in disturbing and humiliating manners. The new entrants to businesses are aware of various dreadful statistics that four-fifth of new businesses will fail within the first two years. Such news is not helping them to venture into their areas of personal interest.

Planning and Preparation

As with any other activity worth winning, planning, and preparing will provide a winning strategy that makes a difference in business. In these times, nothing succeeds without planning.

Most failures are a result of different indices. Indices that could easily be identified, and disaster averted, had adequate measures taken. The importance of planning and preparation cannot be over flogged.

Take a battle, for example, it is a known fact that "there are always two opposing forces that are striving for mastery in other to win. Included also is a battle plan or strategy, as well as the participants involved in a battle with each other. A significant part in putting together a battle plan is taking inventory in order to assess what is needed to win the fight. Those tools along with a plan of execution are crucial for victory. Strategy, the right warfare equipment and the desire for victory are important. Interviews of victorious veterans of war includes roles of faith, endurance, partnership with one another as essential to the success of winning any battle[9]."

The possibility of success and failure will depend on planning, strategy, and attention to detail as in the above war details of a military campaign:

- Having a good plan of action
- Inventorying all you need to succeed
- Knowledge of business

---

[9]Adult Sabbath school study guide, Oct /Nov 2012 Teacher's Edition)

- Available tools
- Persistence and resilience
- Your faith will also be needed to endure hitches during the period.

While statistics may discourage new entrants into business, it can also provide the necessary preparation as they now know what is involved. Running a startup could be pretty tasking yet very rewarding, especially when you invest in a workable strategy, time, finances, and especially viable idea.

Here I suggest to anyone contemplating going into business and hoping to succeed, take a trip to a poultry farm. See for yourself the care and attention given to raising chicks to maturity, and eventually, the sales outlet. The farmer considers everything, including room temperature, vaccines, antibiotics, proper and timely feeding. He observes their droppings, feet, feather, and movement to detect any abnormality.

He invites the best hand to diagnose and treat the birds at every stage of growth. He adds vitamins and other medications occasionally and watches the weather condition. He makes sure of adequate water at all times. He allows only specific people with the proper gear to enter his poultry.

He is careful about the shoes, clothes, grain bags, equipment, and crates he brings inside the poultry. This is because of the possibility that these materials may have come in contact with viruses, bacteria, and other infections. He also knows the implications of exposing such contaminated materials. Such materials can bring in disease or infection that, in one swoop, might wipe away all his investment.

It is the fear of losing the investment that motivates the poultry farmer to pay such detailed attention. These fears advance his farm and earn him profit as the poultry is well taken care of, resulting in high yield.

Managing businesses is not different. No one invests their resources into a business and allows it to waste. Failure to give in time to management will further assert the business failure statistics index. Fear of failure should cause you to be cautious, paying more attention to the business.

In his book, "The impossible is possible, Doing what others says can't be done," John Mason writes about the Chinese Bamboo:

"In the far east, people plant a tree called Chinese Bamboo. During the first four years they water and fertilize the plant with seemingly little results. Then in the fifth year, they again apply water and fertilizer, and in five weeks' time the tree grows ninety feet in height!

Did the Chinese Bamboo tree grow ninety feet in five weeks or five years?

If at any time during these five years the people had stopped watering and fertilizing the tree, it would have died".

Business is not like the tap running into your home that you open and turn off whenever you chose. The fundamental truth is that even with the tap in your home, someone somewhere is working to ensure that the water is treated properly and flows regularly. As you contemplate starting your business, remember the poultry farmer and his birds. Do not also forget the making of the Chinese Bamboo and keep in mind efforts to achieve victory in a military campaign!

Often the difference between success and failure lies in paying attention to details by going the extra mile while not despairing. Both the lady who stayed and did her aptitude test and the one who left must have learned that perhaps in a thousand lies about fifteen percent chance of success. You have to go for that fifteen percent chance of success with every commitment you can muster, even if it means going it over and over again. You must keep in mind that whatever that is worth doing is worth doing well.

With painstaking efforts, purposeful planning, and boldness amid towering challenges, a great mountain will be conquered. As we say in my old neighborhood, "it is always with daring that the little squirrel climbs the length and breadth of the mighty Iroko tree, empty handed".

Yes, that little seedling held its ground that became the great iroko tree that provides shade, shelter, and habitat for ants, birds, animals, and man. You can be the seedling that will become the huge iroko tree tomorrow.

Chapter 7

THE FIRST FIFTEEN YEARS CIRCLE OF DISTINCTION; CREATING YOUR PURPOSE

I will prepare and someday

My chance will come.

-Abraham Lincoln.

Given loads of easily accessible information at our fingertips, it is easier to become successful today. This also leaves us with a deliberate and intentional role to play to find purpose, be more committed and better focused while shutting out distraction seeking our attention.

This is an era of unprecedented access to information, where information has become the new currency of the world. The world as a whole can be traversed and navigated as we relax in the comfort of our homes. We can transact multimillion Dollar business from our Farm, office, car, restroom, and even on transit. Equipped with our Tablets, Ipad, iPhone, Android, Palmtop, Laptop, Notebooks, and other smartphone devices and recently with devices like smartwatches and smart wrist or even smart Television.

What we can achieve through these classy but straightforward toys using eBay, fiber.com, internet marketing, affiliate marketing, joint venture webinar, Amazon, YouTube, Facebook, Whatsapp, Twitter, Email, LinkedIn, the list is endless. All that is needed is the boldness to take the initiative and click the start button of our desired expectations!

Born at the later turn of the 20th Century, I am excited and marveled to have been born at that time of earth history. Having also witnessed in mature glare, significant transformations as the 20th Century rolled to 21st Century with the airplane, electric cars and trains, submarine, wonder drugs, night vision goggles, computers, internet, social media, robotics, communication devices, and other great inventions accomplished.

In this same era, other inventions were improved upon as the entire globe became a highly digital space of bridged international boundaries. Things earlier considered a luxury, only affordable to the rich and super-wealthy, became available even to the common man on the streets and remote areas. It is a privilege to witness changes in trends and shifts in lifestyle.

These changes are seen in music, culture, language, technology, and various other areas of human invention. It will be a great privilege as I hope to know, witness fully, or in part, what the next fifty years will have in its store. Who knows, the next fifty years may give a peep of what the 22nd Century will have in store for that generation. Yes, we are genuinely born at a unique time in earth history.

Wealth creation has been so exposed that minds that hunger and thirst can quickly get it in our current era. Studies have revealed that we do not always need to be extremely talented to be geniuses. We need interest, commitment, hard work, and more hard work to be exceptional. Our preparedness will unleash opportunities.

Malcolm Gladwell, in his book, Outliers, put it bluntly "ten thousand hours spread roughly within ten years is the magic number of greatness." Gladwell maintains that ten thousand hours of constant and dedicated practice with the best hand and facilities will unleash the genius in all of us when given the opportunity of a learning environment in our areas of interest, that is, when we want to be exceptionally good as a writer, basketball player, concert pianist, footballer, Ballerina and in every other area of our chosen interest. According to Malcolm Gladwell, the Outliers may have reached their lofty status through a combination of ability, opportunity, and utterly arbitrary advantage.

I will immediately add that such an advantage comes when you have a conviction of what you want to do and willing to prepare and get absorbed in it. Great accomplishment stems from opportunities taken at perfect timing, borne out of preparedness and purpose.

It is only through a purpose-driven action that motions become progressive. Opportunities do not always wait; the right activities taking at the wrong time is as bad as a terrible decision. Time for investment, growth, and development must be identified, explored, activated, and nurtured. Whatever you do, time will keep ticking away. It never waits. You will not be here forever!

So what is the importance of the first fifteen years after graduation? As small a figure as it looks, fifteen years is a very long period in man's life; this is a period of tremendous growth.

The first fifteen years I am talking about here is the first fifteen years after graduation. It is a time of humble beginning which climax between age thirty-five and forty.

I use graduation, meaning that it does not matter the type of education you acquired your knowledge or skill. It could be a seminary, University, Polytechnic, college of education, training and research centers, Police or Military Academies. It could also be your qualification from other informal vocational training institutes or skill acquisition centers.

It could be on the day you are certified to practice as a fashion designer, auto mechanic, furniture maker, trader, fisherman, barber, driver, cook, dancer, or whatever vocation you chose. The first fifteen years after your qualification or graduation is often a period filled with activities.

The first fifteen years after qualification is an essential phase in your life. The earlier the first fifteen years after graduation to your earlier youthful age, the better. This means that if you graduate between ages twenty to twenty-three, the better.

In Nigeria, for example, it is becoming challenging to gain admission to public universities. Simultaneously, the government tries to reduce this burden by allowing more private institutions, building more federal and state universities.

These public universities, which ought to be affordable and have the capacity to offer admission to more students, in their bid to get more qualified students, they seem to be creating more huddles like the post University matriculation Examination (UME) which sometimes, hinder easy access to gaining admissions in the institution.

Some institutions avoid repeated Joint Admission and Matriculation Board (JAMB) exams and post University Matriculation Examination (UME), and even acing the exams do not guarantee admissions.

Attending private universities means high tuition making it unaffordable to the ordinary children. These challenges make it more difficult to graduate and do the mandatory one-year national youth service, a requirement to get a job before or by the age of twenty-five.

Interestingly, most organizations, especially private firms and other organized sectors willing to employ fresh graduates, usually specify that these young people must not be more than twenty-five years of age at the time of employment.

Considering the challenges of gaining admission to various tertiary institutions, one will need to acquire a skill if your parents can afford it or get a job before proceeding to the higher institution in other to raise money for tuition, which invariably means that most young people gain admission into the tertiary institution between the age of twenty and twenty-five years. This implies that for the majority, meeting the twenty-five years, fresh graduates employable age is out of the way.

Let us also assume that to beat this twenty-five-year challenge, you decide to go for a two-year program. If you do that and you are lucky to secure a job, then proceed to get Higher National Diploma, a Degree or Post Graduate Degree either through part-time weekend programs, evening program, summer program, Open University program, or other avenues.

The establishment you are working with, be it government or private organization, will most likely not accept the new upgrade. They will insist you continue working with the lower qualification you were employed with or resign and re-apply with your new capability, resign and apply for a job that is not available.

The challenge will now be to either continue working on your lower grade with your lower qualification or stuff your upgraded certificate safely in your lock and key. In contrast, the organization you work with benefits from your advance acquired knowledge without commiserate pay.

Alternatively, you have to resign and join the labor market search for a few jobs already overloaded with millions of others already in line with the same or even more advanced qualifications. Therefore, the system takes advantage of job seekers' sea and gets cheap labor with advanced skills without paying for it.

The essence of the above knowledge and exposure is to serve as a call to action for proactive, pragmatic, and strategic thinking for a solution through entrepreneurship.

However, let me be a little generous and hope that majority finish their Higher National Diploma or First Degree by twenty-five years. This could mean that in your first fifteen years after graduation, you will be forty years old!

Remember that there is already an existing argument and myth about age forty. Some believe that a fool at forty is a fool forever, while others think that life begins at forty.

But it is important to stress that whenever a man wakes from his slumber, that becomes his morning; that is to say that what is important is when you get hold of your focus.

Just remember that the first fifteen years after your qualification matters a lot in your life. It is here you will live, grow, and have your being. It is within this period that the totality of your educational investment, life, and work experiences, will be measured and appraised.

The first fifteen years is that period of your life loaded with activities and experiences; challenges, failures, promotions, and peak performances.

It is at this stage that you have to receive more training, specialization, set up your first business, take risks, change jobs, make tremendous and out of the box decisions, make blunders, poor judgments and correct them, climb the ladder of your career, attain positions, marry, have kids, and gather experiences that will guide and provide stability for your second fifteen years.

The second fifteen years are when you receive the gains from your first fifteen years' investments or experiences. Here is a period to consolidate on gains and opportunities for the first fifteen years.

Now assuming you were unable to utilize your first fifteen years, you still have another window of opportunity in your second fifteen years, which will bring you to your fifty-fifth birthday. Hopefully, you are becoming aware that your active years are gradually taking a downward curve at this stage.

In our busy and tight schedules, even our twenty-four-hours-a-day a seem not enough to do all we often intend to, so don't think you do not have time to improve further or take that additional responsibility. Such time will never come.

You must create space to accommodate opportunities that come your way at those fertile periods of your life.

As much as the first fifteen years after your first degree, first diploma or training is important in life. It does not mean that if one misses out in that time of life, the door of opportunities closes.

This is not my intention. We all know many late bloomers, who became successful in their forties, fifties, and even sixties.

This book has stories of successful late starters who conquered at their later time of life. Life is all about boldness, boldness to take up on your dreams, ideas, and aspirations. You can dare life's challenges.

The consequence resulting from that which defies solutions often compel men to conceive and generates its solution. Yes, dire or uncomfortable circumstances should never be seen as an excuse for failure. They provide the zeal and resolve to succeed. It is common knowledge that life-threatening situations spurs men to action and help produce incredible results. This means that you can turn your challenges around to become an asset, which will motivate you to succeed or provide insight into solutions.

You can be who you want to be at any time in your life. Whenever you get hold of yourself, take that bold action and lunch yourself towards your desired destiny, for our actions and commitments could create futures!

Never forget that the first fifteen years after your graduation is the period of an explosion of activities. It could be the most fertile period of your advancement; strive to utilize it meaningfully.

Take that business risk, change jobs, go on that business trip or retreat. If you have not yet secured a position, keep training, retrain, acquire skills, develop yourself, get functional education, get your post-graduate degrees, go for vocational training, and set up a start-up.

I have a saying that 'old age compels the tiger to eat frog.' You must prepare for such time to avoid eating a frog in later years when your strength is weak or diminishing. The opportunity, it is said, favors those that are prepared.

The future belongs to the bold, those who strive to be daring! An opportunity will come one day, be prepared so you will be ready for it when it arrives.

The worst day of your life is when that out-of-the-box opportunity comes. You realized that you are unqualified to take it, especially when you become aware you had had ample time and opportunity to have gotten prepared.

Do not waste this fertile period. You must keep developing yourself at this stage of your life.

The third fifteen years, which brings you to your seventieth birthday, you should be aware time is closing in on you. Make every effort to be the best in what you do but remember when excellence, hard work, and acquired skills meet. Good fortune always seeks you out of the crowd.

Teach your child, student, friend, colleague, and acquaintance the importance of securing a better future by properly harnessing their potentials, especially in their first Fifteen years after graduation.

Remember, in the journey of a successful future, time is of the essence, and as such, it should be adequately planned. Close this book briefly; meditate for fifteen minutes, how your past fifteen years have been and how you intend to pursue it in this period that follows the lockdown.

Now imagine all you can achieve in your next fifteen years. Your life can begin to have a new perspective. You can succeed beyond your imaginations if you dare. You can unleash the entrepreneur in you and reach that desired height!

Chapter 8

DANGEROUS DELAYS –BE DECISIVE

The best years of your life
Are the ones in which you decided
That your problems are your own
You don't blame them on your Mother
The ecology and the President
You realized you control your destiny
-Albert Ellis

I had stopped over at my sister's fashion home that afternoon. There sitting unusually quiet and lost in thought, was one of her customers- turned-friend. That woman, at best, was extrovert and at least extremely playful. She almost didn't notice when I walked in.

We have met on previous occasions. A very cheerful fellow, and with her, there is rarely a dull moment. She keeps people pleasant and laughing, but she was as cold as one who participated in Antarctica's ice bucket challenge on this particular day.

She was on that day out of herself. I thought she might have lost someone dear to her. However, she was reluctant to open up when I enquired about her unusual and cold mood until my sister urged her on.

She had stopped over at her favorite restaurant to have lunch. While she was having her lunch, four individuals, in her word 'corporate looking fellows,' three gentlemen and a lady walked into the same restaurant.

The lady was instantly familiar, like someone from the distant past. Like her usual self, she approached the lady. It turned out that they were classmates in secondary school. They hugged and exchanged pleasantry as their usual old school banter.

This corporate dressed woman (let's call her Jacqueline) was the head of a department in one of the country's leading universities. She already bagged her Ph.D. and married with two kids who were studying abroad.

The irony to her is Jacqueline, who had gone ahead to earn a Ph.D., was, according to her, the 'dunce and blockhead in the blockhead. They had a name for her back then because of her poor academic performance.

Dr. Jacqueline didn't make all her papers during her O-level, while Becky made all her papers at a sitting! Yet Jacqueline has overcome her academic challenges and become a career academician. At the same time, Becky, the bright one in their class, stopped at secondary education.

She got married immediately, hoping to continue her education later, but her dreams were quashed after four children. Unstable income, coupled with family demands over the cause of time, hindered that dream.

Seeing her classmate triggered a thought of the dream she had to shelve, had she not hurriedly gotten married, which was a decision that altered the cause of her life and that of her children. She wondered loudly how Jacqueline, the least bright student in her class, was able to turn her fortune around.

The decision made by Becky and Jacqueline arose from how each of them saw those 48 months it takes to acquire a university degree. Despite academic struggle or getting married first due to financial challenges, earning a degree was the foundation on how each of their fortunes materialized or fell apart.

Beneath the surface lie their levels of persistence. One despaired while another found a reason for motivation despite the failed attempt. It may have taken Jacqueline commitments of more studies and years of taking and retaking high school exams or University exams to finally secure admission to the University.

Both women decided based on what they considered a core priority at that moment, which affected their differed achievements by extension the second fifteen years of their life. How it turned out in the future, which today has become the present, could have been predicted from mere deductive reasoning.

Decision making is vital to the growth and progress of any individual, family, organization, or country. You are products of your choices and decisions. These decisions would make or mar you if not now, then, in the future.

It is important to make a significant decision with a long-term view. If you chose not, whatever outcome becomes your decision, for lack of judgment is in itself a decision. You are safer and better when you make a favorable decision.

In making any decision, one needs to be thorough, well informed, experienced, confident, and knowledgeable on the issue. It is always profitable to see the bigger picture beyond the narrow gaze of the moment.

Decisions can be made at the spur of the moment like in emergencies, yet we must note that decisions, especially those relating to the future, should not be influenced by current challenges. We can, in that circumstance, see a more splendid future ahead if we are hopeful.

When we try to see the picture as a whole and not in part, it is then that we can work through current challenges and circumstances as we treat such situations precisely what they are -a passing phase because phases come and goes. Becky decided to get married without considering the bigger picture, the future; instead, she made decisions based on fear.

Mistakes are bound to be made when you lack the foresight to see through the veil to the bigger picture.

The story of the ten blind men of India readily comes to mind. They described an elephant based on the part of its body, each touched, neglecting that the parts can never be equal to the sum of its whole.

Years back, when I and some of my friends were still single, I worked in different organizations, businesses, and other states. We found ourselves in a particular city on a few occasions, either on a business trip or official duty. The friend whose city we were visiting hosts us. This could happen twice a year that business or official duty coincidentally took all or four of us to a particular state where one of us resided same time.

In such time our host could treat us to lunch or dinner depending on the time and engagement. We prepare the meals together, and we would delve into various discussions. Those discussions were tagged Men's Forum, Guys Forum, or One on One Forum.

On a particular occasion, we were joined by another friend of ours who coincidentally in that town. At another event, we had a very bright and intelligent lady who participated in our Guys Forum. Both easily got assimilated into our discussions.

We thought it would be rewarding to have a lady's perspective on various male issues, so she was admitted. She was overwhelmed by the blunt no-hold-back guy's perspective on issues at the forum.

Guys' forum was a time we usually looked up to, though never planned, such became a time to catch up on old gist and update each other with plans and program that wouldn't have been thoroughly discussed over phone as we vet and gave suggestions. Our discussions were more centered on relationships, career paths and national issues often political. We latter nicknamed the occasion 'Guys forum-One on One.

The forum had no moderator issues discussed include career, relationships, politics, religion, contemporary and current trending issues making the news. We also used the opportunity to appraise each other. We shared sensitive relationship issues, how each was faring or needed improving, and of course, jokes and 'yab'[10].

Our unwritten code was that nothing each said, questions asked, or suggestions are given during Guys Forum: One-on-One was considered offensive or too intrusive.

Everyone has expected, if need be, to be blunt in questions, no-hold-back, logical, and objective, answers were expected at all times.

On this particular day, while discussing relationships, one of us had asked a question directed at no one in particular "If fortune swings at either of us tomorrow and you become a governor, country's' President or another Mark Zuckerberg in your line of business, will you be comfortable with the partner you are currently dating. If you both get married because of position at the moment, will you be pleased with her as the first lady? It was a call to looking inward at the bigger picture beyond the limitations of the moment.

But this was a question few of us never considered until that point in time. As harmless and straightforward as the question sounds, those in doubt about their relationship took a long time, giving a straight yes or no answer to the problem.

It was food for thought for us group members. One of us later ended a relationship as he could not provide a self-satisfactory and

---

[10] *friendly jest*

comfortable answer. At the same time, that question strengthened another's relationship.

When we are thorough in our decision, we can be confident to take whatever outcome, knowing we gave our best shot based on information available to us at that particular time.

Unfortunately, not all of our decisions will always turn outright. Even with our best intentions, our choices may end up being imperfect. However, this should not deter us, knowing that we gave our best in that given situation from options available.

A decision is a choice of logical selection from options available to us after thinking through what will be in our best interest at a given time. It infers choosing the best from various alternatives. In decision making, options are weighed before concluding. While some decisions will take time to arrive, others may need to be taken at the spur of the moment.

At other times decisions are influenced by our past or present experiences or out of intuition and by gathering information from different sources.

Medical doctors, for example, make decisions from their learning and past experiences as professionals. Sometimes, they gather information from their professional colleagues and organizations across the globe.

Experienced drivers have been able to avert what would have been fatal accidents, sometimes judging the situation and slowing down. They intuitively know when a careless driver will overtake or when a child will likely run across the road, chasing a ball, pet, or friends that have crossed the road ahead of them.

In making decisions out of intuition, we sometimes hear comments like

- I feel it in my bones that I will get this job
- I just have this gut feeling I will win the lottery

- I feel this sensation as if something terrible is about to happen
- I just knew this business would be a hit. I can even see it in my mind's eye
- I hear inner voices

A friend told me an experience he had while on a military assignment amid night patrol during a peacekeeping assignment in another country. For no reason, he felt like he's being hounded and stalked, it was at the dead of the night, and for no reason, he dived behind a rock, right at that time and spot, firearms exploded, shattering and reaping apart everything on its way. He reacted out of intuition, and that reaction saved his life.

Whether we make decisions out of logic, knowledge, intuition, professional experience, or experience gathered from different sources, our brain's power is always on alert in case duty calls. The mind remains the most important system in information processing and decision making.

The human brain is a very complex, multifaceted, but exciting system. We need to pay attention and learn some of its unique capabilities. You don't need to be a brain surgeon, medical, or health personnel to know the brain's essential functions, especially regarding decision making.

Here is a view of the two parts of the brain and how it functions and helps in decision making:

Right Hemisphere

The Quick Facts

Functions: Responsible for control of the left side of the body, and is the more artistic and creative side of the brain

Left Hemisphere

The Quick Facts

Functions: Responsible for control of the right side of the body, and is the more academic and logical side of

the brain

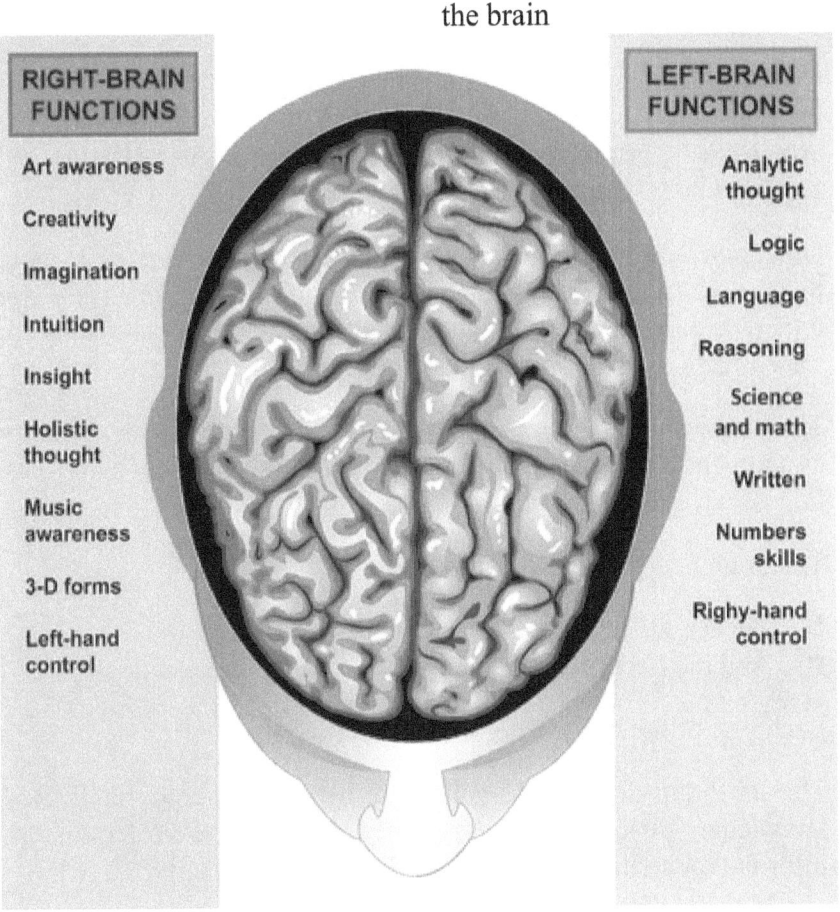

RIGHT-BRAIN FUNCTIONS

Art awareness

Creativity

Imagination

Intuition

Insight

Holistic thought

Music awareness

3-D forms

Left-hand control

LEFT-BRAIN FUNCTIONS

Analytic thought

Logic

Language

Reasoning

Science and math

Written

Numbers skills

Righy-hand control

If you split the brain right down the middle into two symmetrical or equal parts, you would have a right and left hemisphere. Although similar in size, these two sides are not the same and do not carry out the same functions.

The left side of the brain is responsible for controlling the right side of the body. It also performs tasks that have to do with logic, such as in science and mathematics.

On the other hand, the right hemisphere coordinates the left side of the body and performs tasks that have to do with creativity and the arts. Both hemispheres are connected by the corpus callosum and serve the body in different ways[11].

Our brain is a very complex machine that can do things far more than our wildest imaginations. Paying attention leads to understanding our mind and what it unconsciously tells or transmits to us through our body systems.

The brain's intuitive power is why the friend on military assignment could react and obey his intuition spontaneously. This, in turn, saved his life.

The brain is divided into two parts.

- The Right Hemisphere
- And the Left hemisphere

Each part of the brain deals with a specific job.

The left brain or the left hemisphere handles concrete intellectual knowledge. In solving problems, the left hemisphere offers factual information related to the topic of discussion uniquely.

On the other hand, the right brain or right hemisphere deals with the abstract that cannot be expressed by words. That is where intuition comes in.[12] The feeling that something is about to happen. This part of the brain reaches into our subconscious mind. It can come up with concrete answers based on a much wider pool of information than the rational fact. When you use such words as a gut feeling, inner voices, I sensed that, etc.

---

[11]brainmadesimple.com/left-and-right-hemisphere.html

[12]Elise Lebeau

Sometimes you trust these feelings even when you cannot logically explain them. Decision making will be significantly improved if the two parts of the brain are called to action while deciding by using both parts frequently.

We need to pay attention to our senses. They are always transmitting information to us, but often we ignore them till it happens.

These two parts of the brain are interdependent and ensure survival. Our intuitive, logical, and factual brain can provide a healthy balance that improves decision-making quality.

It is being said that women are more intuitive while men are more logical. Using the two parts of the brain in our decisions will empower growth in every area of our life.

In making decisions, we must pay attention to our ideas, suggestions, and senses to compare gathered information.

Understandably people vary when it comes to making decisions. Some people take much time to conclude. They sleep over it, discuss it with friends, colleagues, family members, or fellow professionals. In contrast, others are quick at arriving at a decision.

In making decisions, you must be thorough, weigh the pros and cons and consequences of the decision you are about to take in your life and that of others.

It is becoming imperative to make decisions quickly and on time in our highly interconnected world. In this fast-paced world of business, the faster the decision, the better.

Time and planning are crucial in achieving set goals, beat the competition, meet targets, conclude negotiation, close deals, and deliver sales.

In some countries where the environment can be volatile and unpredictable due to the sudden movement of events, religious crises, terrorism, corruption, security challenges, and unstable government policies, even a well-informed decision can overnight be turned on its head.

In the zeal to safeguard life and proper plans, plans are abandoned as people may be forced to relocate to other parts of the country or part of the world a few weeks or months after investing their life savings in a business they were cocksure succeed.

They abandon these investments and move to other areas to be assured of relative peace and safety. In these troubling times, these unexpected challenges have caused the right decisions to fail.

We may foretell the future, although we cannot predict with accuracy the turn of events. As such, some decisions though they failed, cannot be called a wrong decision. This is because they were made with the best information available at that particular time. It turned bad does not make it the wrong decision.

Consider well-thought plans and effective decisions and plans made before the coronavirus pandemic was unleashed on our earth with a lockdown that has impacted our choices negatively. Those couldn't have been said to be bad decisions.

In making decisions, we must consider its impact on ourselves, family, colleagues, environment, country, and the world.

Man being part of a global village, decisions made in the United States of America or China can have consequences worldwide. These also may mean that decisions in Africa or other countries can have a global impact. We have seen how troubled countries like Syria have thrown refugee problems across Europe and different western world.

Financial decisions made in one country can spiral into an economic depression that might engulf the entire world just as the decision in a country's foreign policy or natural resources can positively or negatively affect another part of the world.

There are times we must be very decisive and bold enough to make a monumental decision without consulting anyone. Such determination must be made at the spur of the moment to save life or organization. In such a situation, experience comes to bear. Pilots, parents, medical personnel, firefighters, corporate executives, teachers, individuals, and entrepreneurs are expected to be very decisive at such times. Such moments make or break an organization, an individual, or a service.

Right decisions have made people reach out to the stars in glory. In contrast, the terrible decision has reduced people to penury, mortgaged nations into perpetual debt, abject poverty, pain, and suffering. Some decisions have led countries to avoidable wars.

Right decisions have seen countries within a few decades' leap ahead of their contemporaries in development. Some Asian countries provide the world with a model of how the right decision can spearhead chains of developmental strategies and strides. These decisions had put them ages ahead of their contemporaries in a short time.

Some parents have made decisions that enslave the entire family and cause enmity and feuds between families even before their children's birth.

Some families have moved far ahead due to the right decisions, and graduates have moved far beyond their peers due to superior decisions.

In homes, parents should allow their children to be involved in decision making from a tender age. They should be allowed to identify mistakes when made, correct, and bear some consequences of bad decisions.

Usually, when children are younger, their parents make most of the decisions. As they grow, the parents gradually withdraw and relinquish some of the findings. As they grow into adolescents and teenagers, more opportunities are allowed them to make decisions.

Here, parents may trust them to make better and informed decisions on their own.

The effectiveness of these teenagers or younger adults' decisions will be determined by the quality of positive advice, choices, and mental attitude they have been exposed to growing up.

Young people contemplating marriage have the burden to decide on the partner's personality they wish to spend the rest of their life.

They often consider individual temperament, religion, compatibility, family traits, and management of finances, hobbies, and other attributes while making these decisions.

Failure to make the right marital decisions will be akin to the proverbial living on rooftops to avoid domestic chaos. Such marriages have resulted in divorce, broken homes, and depression. Children are worse hit in troubled families.

I once heard that everything is given to achieve victory in war. People make very dangerous and sometimes inhuman decisions, affect lives, and leave both parties hurting, wounded, and disillusioned many years after the war campaign has ended.

War does not profit either the victor and especially not to the vanquished. The world is yet to recover from decisions made in past wars and battles. Such includes:

- Nigerian-Biafra civil war
- America's military campaign in Vietnam and Iraq
- Bombing of Japanese cities of Hiroshima with Uranium gun-type atomic bomb (little man) and Nagasaki with plutonium

implosion-type bomb (fat man) both of which were said to kill over 226,000 people, mainly civilians

- Rwandan genocides
- Sierra Leone blood diamond
- Israeli-Lebanese conflicts
- Arab springs in Egypt, Libya, Syria, and other places are part of decisions and uprisings that will continue to hurt and hunt all parties involved many years after the campaigns had ended.
- And the latest detonation of an impounded shipment of seven-year-old 2750 tons of ammonium nitrate in a Beirut port in Lebanon caused a massive explosion that rocked the city, leaving over 300,000 homeless and hundreds dead and Beirut being declared as a 'disaster city' by the authorities. An explosion that was felt over 150 kilometers to Cyprus.

Being decisive is the characteristic of great leaders. To gain the ability to decide quickly and successfully, it is important to train, learn, and follow your inner voice, intuition, or gut feeling, sometimes called the sixth sense.

More often than not, such decisions are made within the shortest possible time, which may be in a matter of seconds, minutes, or as the situation warrants.

Our brain is wired with the capacity to deliver answers and the right information at excellent speed spot on in moments.

Herbert Douglas's book, How to survive the 21st Century, stated that to be decisive, we must follow these essential habits.

- Listen carefully
- Probe for facts by raising thoughtful questions
- Evaluate information gathered

Douglas went ahead to write that quality of decisiveness begins with the right information gathered. He advanced that with sufficient information, decisive people exhibit certain valuable traits:

- Crispness in speech, conduct, attitude, and conclusions.
- Positive, not arrogance, regarding themselves, their environment, and their values.
- Calm detachment regarding themselves and circumstances.
- They think long-range as they continue to gather and evaluate facts about what matters and require a decision. Need to value time by sticking close to daily, weekly and monthly plans knowing that distraction blurs focus.

Here is a story of a sea captain whose moment of decisiveness at the spur of the moment saved a hopeless situation:

"All summer Dutch Sea Captain John Lindeman took boatloads of rich European sightseers to an uninhabited island to experience the fanfare of an active volcano.

On August 26th, 1883, the little Island, too small to even bother naming on most maps exploded, Captain Lindeman was in the Sunda traits when Krakatoa erupted. Heavy ash and pumice fell on the ship.

The choppy waters made it impossible to land. Early the next morning, the captain watched a wave swept away those gathered on the pier of Telok Betong and beaches a ship among coconut trees.

To save his ship, he dropped both anchors heading straight into the waves.

The crew, passengers, and ship were tossed violently; sulphuric acid burned the air. In ten minutes, the ship's deck was covered in a foot and a half of pumice.

The sea heaved convulsively as they worked desperately to clear the deck. It seems a losing battle, and a killer wall of water came at them. Captain Lindeman lashed himself down in the engine room.

When the monster wave hit, the crew was flung from one side of the engine room to the other. The ship rode up the lock until it was vertical, and the sea sawed down.

The crew and passengers gave up for dead. When the wind died down at around noon, a deadly calm ensued more frightening than the storm. Not one passenger lost his life thanks to the decisiveness of the sea captain who dropped anchor and headed straight into the killer waves". Captain Linderman's determination saved the crew and passengers.

Little wonder Ralph Waldo Emerson penned those words that still rings true to date "once you make a decision, the universe conspires to make it happen." You are to decide and know when to follow your hunch!

The eruption of Krakatau has been classified as the loudest sound on earth. The sound was so loud and was heard more than 3000km away in Perth, and more than 5000km in the opposite direction on Rodriguez's Indian Ocean Island. It blasts ash about 80km into the atmosphere, and ash clouds around the earth, having the power of numerous atomic bombs.

The explosion led to the death of more than 40,000 people. It is estimated that the eruption force was 10,000 times greater than the hydrogen bomb dropped in the city of Hiroshima. The blast's percussive force was so great that it traveled back and forth around the world seven times!

Not long ago, an elderly US woman, Helen Collins, was in an airplane with the husband, a pilot, when the husband, John, suddenly developed a fatal heart attack mid-air.

The 80-year-old Helen, with the help of the control tower and a pilot in another plane hovering and instructing her, decisively took control of the twin-engine Cessna plane in the skies and safely, after a harrowing 90 minutes, landed the airplane. But despite the miracle of a safe landing, her 81-year-old husband, John, did not survive the attack.

Information is power; knowledge and experience will breed confidence that brings about the right decision. Whether you are a driver, businessman, teacher, student, medical professional, or parent, these qualities will make a massive difference in any event.

Chapter 9

WALK THE TALK

How poor are they that have not patience!

What wound did ever heal but by degree

-William Shakespeare

As a graduating senior, I was allowed to speak to the institution's entire faculty and student body. Those years, it was the norm to select few graduating students to speak to the whole student body and faculty.

The range of topics presented by these seniors varied; it may be personal experience, academic or financial challenges, and overcoming such difficulties.

It could be an academic paper presentation, questionnaire, research work, sermon, inspiration or motivational talk, or any topic you find of interest and consider helpful and informative to the academic community.

I had always been interested in managing small scale businesses in the face of massive unemployment. With millions of graduates churned out each year from the higher institutions adding to the number of unemployed youths in the country, no brainer chose a topic.

I resolved to do a research presentation relating to managing small businesses, primarily in developing countries.

The aim was to help equip my fellow grandaunts with options to try new business opportunities for themselves. I set out a research work that can empower and stir others to think about self-reliance and entrepreneurship.

We have been educated from the four walls of the university, academically sound, but that we are equipped enough to translate that knowledge to meet our needs, and that of our society remained to be seen.

In an environment of massive unemployment, it is important to de-emphasize employment instead of emphasizing job creation by graduates. That way, their mindset will start early to be self-reliant even as they seek paid work.

Education should equip and empower an individual with the freedom to exercise the mental skill and knowledge either inherent or acquired by the individual. Such education should help one arrive at an independent conclusion without exclusively basing the decision on an authority's verdict.

Regrettably, education has been reduced to an instrument that offers merely the opportunity for a graduate to get a good-paying job and live comfortably ever after; a purpose education has failed to accomplish.

In a real sense, education should aim to empower, equip, and position man to think and develop himself by creating ideas that can translate to services, products, or equipment—utilizing his mental capabilities to pursue and achieve that which his mind conceives, for his benefit and that of society.

Education ought to be a continuous improvement of the individual to acquire knowledge and value for life skills and purposeful living. An instrument that breeds continuous development and empowers one, especially after leaving the walls of academia. It should aim to stir the progressive development of mind and character to achieve its potentials.

Education can be received through training in formal or informal settings - the Universities, Research Centers, Polytechnics, colleges, and other Institutions or bypassing skills through vocations or apprenticeship.

Proper education should identify and help a child discover his distinctive potential and master such proficiencies.

Unfortunately, education often is and solely academics. Our contemporary education would have killed great footballers' extraordinary skills as Jay-Jay Okocha, Kanu Nwankwo. It would have wiped out the gift and talent of music maestros 50 Cents, Jay Z, and mastery of standup comedians like Trevor Noah, Alibaba, Chris Rock, Kevin Harts.

Until lately, our academic education seems to show less importance to skills and talents that may not be based on pure classroom academic work.

Hence such education had failed in helping students discover their latent potentials and interest, which often leaves graduates in self-doubts and totally at the mercy of job-seeking instead of skill acquisition.

Back to my graduating senior presentation, from the responses, standing ovation, and feedback received, it was safe to conclude that the presentation was well-received. My Head of Department greened from ear to ear and requested I send him a copy; of my presentation!

Years after graduation, when I had worked as an employee in different states of the federation and eventually started my own business, I then realized that sometimes no matter how you think you had researched and mastered a topic in the library or an institution, talk can be cheap and field experience could be opposite as it can be parallel.

Life in the field could be similar to an aggressive and venomous snake that crawls into your room in the dark; you have the difficulty of figuring out where the head and tail are situated before attempting fight or flight. Much more is needed in the field.

DETERMINATION, DRIVE, AND MOTIVATION

Although the above three seem alike to drive the point, I chose to treat them separately. Determination is that strength of mind to endure without despair. In it are embedded grit, sacrifice, commitment, and consistency!

Determination is the will never to give up and to persevere. The drive is like the horsepower that propels an engine and provokes motion.

Motivation is like holding on to life support, the little floating object on the sea that must be held to stay floating and alive!

Above dream, idea, knowledge, super product, and available fund, lies bedrocks for success, determination, drive, and motivation. It is a resolve and will to be steadfast, clinical, and consistent in pursuing set goals. Determination is the point where motivation and drive meet.

There are heaps of challenges and distractions; if unprepared, they can rock the business boat. Even your character or attitude could make or wreck a business with great potential for success.

Determination is far more than the icing on a cake. It is the heat without which every preparation, effort dispensed in practice, and baking becomes useless. It is the strength of mind and character to keep going.

Drive can be achieved when there is passion in what you are doing, and this passion motivates even when your resolve runs in short supply.

In the field, I realized that determination, drive, and motivation were three primary attributes I should have mentioned in my graduating class presentation. Unfortunately, this trio, researched from the library, did not give the strength and weight of attention it deserves.

Without the trio, it will be difficult for a start-up to sustain the assault of rough and uncertain business terrain.

Determination, motivation, and drive are the mainstay of the business, especially at incubation.

Determination is that additional or extra step you take when you think you have reached your wit end and exhausted all possibilities. It is that inner strength that exhales when all remedies seem to have failed. Most achievements are actualized as a result of being determined.

Determination is the core attribute for eventual productive performance. An inner drive and willpower keep pushing and stirring you to move on, go a step further, and never quit because you are convinced and confident in your idea.

It is that last rough hedge, after which you strike gold when you may have reached your wit's end. Determination starts at the point of giving up when you are on the threshold of letting go.

Only a few good things in life can be achieved without such resolve. It takes determination to graduate with cum laude, magna cum laude, or summa cum laude. It builds a successful relationship, leads a country, excels in your choosing career or profession.

It promotes scientific breakthrough, wins a championship, and achieve business success. It powers an individual to climb back to success after each douse of disappointment, mistakes, and failures.

It takes determination to write this book. Life's success stories are a product of determination. It is that extra effort invested to achieve a goal in the face of odds and when the future looks bleak.

Years ago, after the Christmas holiday. I was driving back from Aba (Eastern Nigeria) to Kaduna (Northern Nigeria), a journey of about eight hundred and fifty kilometers. This was during the era when bad roads and potholes were the banes of Nigerian roads.

This journey started at about 5:30 am, but the trip was delayed due to occasional heavy traffic congestion. We spent much more time on the road. Fortunately, it was a double lane road. As at 9 pm, I was still on the road, but suddenly thick fog started gathering. The fog was so heavy that one could virtually be tempted to slice through it.

In all its brightness, the car headlamp could not penetrate the fog but for a very short distance. My friends were exhausted and all asleep while I maneuvered through the thick fog of darkness as I made haste slowly.

I considered parking to see if the fog would clear, but the danger of been hit from behind by coming vehicles and being attacked by armed robbers kept me moving.

While the fog was getting thicker as I struggle on the trip, I estimated and discovered I still had about two hours' drive to Kaduna, the final destination.

Visibility was so blurred and low, the only thing the car headlamp could pick a few meters away from where the white stripes at the Centre of the road! So I focused on the stripes while having in mind the long, arduous journey ahead. I drove steadily and at a languid pace, knowing that I could quickly be confronted suddenly with potholes, parked broken down vehicles, and other obstructions.

Using the Centre stripes to determine the road's width, I focused with great concentration and attention until I passed through, away from the thick fog to clear visibility and finally to our destination safely.

My sleeping friends eventually woke up, not knowing what I have been through for over two hours engulfed in an unusual fog!

I bring this experience to explain determination, going steady, maintaining focus, and abhorring distractions. Having in mind your short and long-term goals while holding on to that short ray of hope will eventually lead you safely to your destination even when colleagues, friends, loved ones. Other acquaintances ignore your struggles challenges.

A determined mind will hold out storms of life. He could be bent but never broken, baked, burnt, and delayed, but success is assured.

Being determined is far from being healthy. At some point, the strong do get broken, but the determined has a kind of resilience. When the challenges of life get stormy, like the tough plant, they bend, stretch, and swing with the wind and straightens up soon after the storm is over. They do not despair.

They are patient with life's uncertainties knowing that even though the journey has taken more time than expected, at the least, it will average out. It could mean shedding different kinds of weight when necessary by temporarily giving up comfort for a better outcome tomorrow.

There is an understanding that the fog may be so thick and heavy that you can almost touch it, yet they know like ice, there is always a melting point. Challenges have a life span; with patience, focus, and resilience, it will still be outlived.

However, a determination is meaningless if you are at the wrong destination. You must be sure of what you are pursuing and where you are headed. It would be best if you were cocksure of your great idea; it is when you are sure that your resolve will germinate and flourish.

I read a story in a small book a friend gave me as a present:

It happened in Kent, Washington.

James Wilson decided he wanted a well to argument the water supply on his five-acre tract land. So he hired J.C Maxwell, a professional well-digger, to drill a hole deep into the earth behind Wilson's home and hopefully find water.

It was a Tuesday when the good digger arrived and began to sink his steel shaft into mother earth. Twenty feet down, no water. Fifty feet and still no water.

"Shall I dig on, Mr. Wilson?"

"Of course! We must have water.

Seventy feet down, no water, one hundred feet, no water. Deep and more profound, the metal bit chewed its way to the earth.

One hundred and ninety feet; finally, the drill crunched its way to two hundred feet below the surface. Still no water.

"Farther, Mr. Wilson?"

'Yes!'

At two hundred and ten feet down, there arose from the bosom of the earth a faint and distance sound to the two men high above. It was a deep, throaty gurgling sound of roaring, rushing water! Wilson and Maxwell instinctively stepped back from the hole just in time to witness an explosion of water that shot out of the ground like old faithful herself!

It was a geyser into the sky, and nobody could stop it! Neighbors with shovel were summoned, drainage ditches were dug. A mechanical digger was placed in operation. And still, the water exploded into the heavens from beneath the earth!

They had struck an Artesian Well, and that was on Tuesday. By Wednesday evening, there was such a flood of water that Mr. Wilson called the sheriff for more help. County road equipment was brought in, and irrigation ditches were dug to serve the entire valley. Geologists got onto the scene estimated that water was pouring out of the well at the rate of 1600 gallons per minute! It was an out running of water that they estimated would adequately serve forty-six-thousand persons per day!

They had struck an artesian well! [13]

It takes daring to continue digging amidst challenges. Still, those who hold on will eventually be struck the artesian well of success, which will not only be of benefit to themselves and their families but many others far and near!

---

[13] THE CLAIM, Dwight. k. Nelson. Page 22-23

PART 2

LITTLE THINGS THAT MATTER

Building personal capacity

Some people covet successes; admire budding and thriving business and empires. They envy accomplishments and love people who have triumphed in their chosen undertakings. They identify people who are said to have a special touch and succeed in every endeavor of their choice.

They refer to others as geniuses, corporate giants, Rock star CEOs, Boardroom champions, and the like. They do not often realize that behind that huge visible success and unprecedented achievement lies years of sacrifice, failures, constant pruning, uncertainties, frustrations, near-miss opportunities, self-denials, and about of loss driven by fears at inception or over some time.

They made hard decisions and difficult choices as the consistent efforts trigger leads that eventually generated yields! There is always a price to pay for success, even those who often seem to succeed with little effort. They must have paid the price and learned from it to do better. Yes, success comes with a price that stems from goals, desires, and dreams.

Success doesn't just come; it is a product of deliberate and strategic planning and focused engagements. Success starts from getting the small things right!

These small things are akin to life skills that should be adequately screwed, especially at inception, and oiled continuously to keep the wheel rolling and provide wings with which plans will eventually fly. This section will provide such an aerial view that triggers a deliberate intent to flourish.

Chapter 10

THE NUTS AND BOLTS OF BUSINESS

There is safety in small beginning
And there is unlimited capital
In the experience gain by grouping"
-Henry Ford.

Just before you get started, consider these necessities. These can be said to be the nuts and bolts of the business. Failure to screw them rightly and tightly, all effort will not only crumble, but it will crumble like a pack of cards.

These Tips are nuggets and action points resulting from experiences and research over the cause of doing business. When put into practice will aid you in making your business a delightful experience. These nuggets will help avoid potholes, pitfalls, and other obstacles that would have delayed success or caused business failures. There are more of these tips, but putting all here will make for prolonged reading, so they are compressed to these fourteen easy to recall action points. I am convinced by my experiences and that of my numerous clients that these points will help entrepreneurs:

- Secure a solid base that will engineer and power your new start-up
- Gain you happy clientele
- Improve your productivity
- And effectively promote your general business experience

LOCATION:

When you are convinced of what to establish, whether service business, manufacturing, and merchandise, consider the location, where the business will be established.

Consider demographic, socio-cultural, and political factors relating to your business. Is it close to your sources of raw materials? What is your customer base in that environment? Who are you targeting - infant, children of school age, adult, household, educational institutions, farmers, and government establishments?

Remember, general overhead cost varies from one location to another. Consider the cost of doing business in each environment. The local environment provides peculiar challenges as much in varying degrees to the metropolis. Identify these unique and eculiar challenges.

While available infrastructures are not a challenge in the urbane environment, this could not be entirely in villages. You may provide your source of power supply, create an access road, provide your security, communication, or internet facility, or even water requirement to run your business.

Are your customers located within your vicinity, or you will need to go out to reach them. Will the place be temporary or permanent? Experience shows that it is unhealthy to keep moving your business location because while you lose some of your customers, it also portrays inconsistency.

COMPETITION:

Consider the competition in your chosen location. A stiff competition or an already established competitor may prove a difficult challenge for your new business. This is because those businesses are already well established and more financially stable with a strong customer base. They control the prices of products far beyond what your limited fund can put up with.

Penetrating the same market may prove challenging unless you are coming with more innovative ideas and better products than your competitors. Even when that is the case, you will still need more marketing, which could be expensive for your start-up budget. But it's all about strategy. Healthy competition needs to meet with a better winning strategy. At other times it should inspire you to do more and to be at your toes always.

However, suppose you can't swim with the big fishes. In that case, your new business will be better off if established in an environment with less competition. Unless you can make do with the crumbs, I doubt if any business is started with a crumb mindset. Yours shouldn't.

Do you trust your idea or product enough to share the market space with already existing firms? Can your work be good enough to challenge existing ones and attract some of their customers to you? These are the issues you must consider. Know your competitors and know what you are bringing into the market to challenge that market.

FUNDING:

Consider sources of funding for the new business. How to raise funds for start-up capital yet sustain self in that early stage of the business? Consider starting with a personal fund as an investment seed to avoid the pressure of paying back. It is often a long, tough call. The business strives to gather speed in performance, become self-sufficient, and start making a profit. This usually takes time. If you decide to take a loan, try and make such loans on a long-term repayment plan so your business will not be under the pressure of interests and repayment in the short term.

Consider raising capital first from personal funds, family members, friends, associations, or corporative societies or seeking to attract investors and loans from banks.

Attracting investors will involve writing a business plan. Most people shy away from writing business plans for various reasons; they think it's complicated and ambiguous. They assume it's difficult to write a winning business plan, and it takes lots of professionalism to write one. Others see a business plan as a detailed, time-consuming document that is needed only when sourcing for funds.

Of course, a business plan is essential when sourcing funds, yet it goes beyond that. It helps you put your business in a proper perspective, which will also help reduce business failure.

Business plan

A business plan is a written document describing the business's nature, the sales and marketing strategy, and the financial background. It contains a projected profit and loss statement. It is a road map that provides directions, so a business can plan the future to avoid bumps in the road. The time you spend making your business plan thorough and accurate and keeping it up-to-date is an investment that pays big dividends in the long term[14].

Develop a winning business plan that meets generally accepted guidelines and help you overcome future business hurdles. Today, information can be gotten at the tip of the fingertip through your smartphone and other devices. Your business plan should conform to generally accepted guidelines regarding form and content. Each section should include specific elements, addresses, and relevant questions that the people who read your project will most likely ask. Some people think you don't need a business plan unless you're trying to borrow money. Of course, you do indeed need a good strategy if you intend to approach a lender--whether a banker, a venture capitalist, or any number of other sources for start-up capital. A business plan is more than a pitch for financing; it's a guide to help you define and meet your business goals[15].

STAFFING/MANPOWER:

Hiring staff for business is a needful area that should not be taken for granted. Often an entrepreneur is as good as his business, and

---

[14] *Small business encyclopedia.*
[15] www.entrpreneur.com

his company is as good as its staff. It's all interwoven. The need to employ those who have a passion for following the business owner's vision becomes paramount. This is especially the case at the earlier stage of the business as the owner seeks to establish the trend and image the company is to be known.

In grooming staff initially, a lot will depend on the business owner; it is essential to lead by example. The passion you have for your new business will bring motivation to your staff.

As a start-up, the business owner should not ask staff to be punctual and then strolls in aimlessly and randomly at any time of the day. Employees consciously and unconsciously act according to how they see or perceive owners' commitment.

A variety of other factors inspires business success. This includes hard work, a positive attitude from its owner, and an amalgamation of varying factors; attention to detail, strategic marketing, good working condition, respect to staff and clients, a winning product, a conscious and deliberate effort to succeed. When the owner gets it right in these areas at the early stages, it inadvertently rubs off on the staff to the extent that even in the owner's absence, the employees act in that line of commitment.

I have often seen business owners whose lifestyles are at variance with their goals and objectives. The business will most likely fail due to poor management than due to low funds.

Have a good knowledge of your business yet employ those better than you in specific areas. The old axiom has it that you have monkeys as staff when you pay peanut – this still holds to date.

MARKETING:

As a start-up, do not underestimate the power of marketing. It could be a word of mouth, one-on-one direct marketing strategy. This is a cost-effective strategy that gets your product or idea known to friends, neighbors, colleagues, and other users. This is where the strength of your social capital will be of great advantage.

A rich social capital will provide initial connection and means of getting the knowledge of your products out to the public. It will also bring the referral, and referral is the meat of marketing. People tend to value products recommended by someone they know or someone who had used the product. Take advantage of the power of your social capital. Your marketing begins with those around you.

In this era of opportunities, the world has gone digital, where we find ourselves engaged daily in online activities. Digital marketing is a profit-generating platform on the loose these times. Resolve to create leads and clientele through this medium. Businesses can take advantage of various social media platforms and ads to generate massive leads that will trigger sales. Invest and learn to use multiple internet-based platforms. The internet and social media advert provide immense opportunities to bring clients to your business. This will be discussed in subsequent chapters.

You can also employ the services of professional marketers using different marketing strategies. This could be paid advert in newspapers, magazines, radio, and television. Other mass media agencies and public relations channels that could be employed to get your product to public awareness include trade shows, promotions, seminars, and workshops.

Marketing is successful if it can persuade consumers to choose your product even when there are alternative products from competitors.

A business owner can also go into marketing before the arrival of his product to the market. This brings awareness of the incoming new product before it makes its physical presence in the market. Such action keeps consumers in anticipation of the work.

Just as your product and your employees are needed, your business life's success will depend heavily on your marketing strategy.

A right product that is unknown is as good as nonexistent. A suitable product that consumers are not aware of its benefits will fail. An average yield that is well marketed will continue to take massive market share and sells more than an excellent product that is not well marketed. The average work will continue to hold sway in the market until the good one is introduced and adequately dealt with. A good product left on shelve is of no value to both the inventor and others.

As a new business, it is essential to identify various users of your product. Also, identify non-users, low users, and significant users to concentrate your effort initially on major users. This strategy will cut down the cost of marketing and reduce your overhead cost. By this act, you utilize your limited resources efficiently and effectively.

As a business grows and starts paying its bills and making profits, there is the need to revisit the low users and non-users and educate them on the benefits they will gain from using your product. Educating users about your products provide answers about the new product or service you are offering, its uniqueness, and why it is a better alternative than what they are already used to. These advantages needs are emphasized.

Successful marketing involves knowing your product in and out. People will have more confidence in the product if they know you and your organization uses your product, especially where your product is what you can use. They also become more comfortable when products are recommended by someone they knew. Sometimes I stop using products when I found out that some of the company's staff patronize most of their competitors. It shows me that the other products are better than theirs.

OFFICE AND EQUIPMENT:

As a new business, cutting down costs and managing the scarce fund and other resources are necessary. Ask yourself if you will pay for office space, work from your vehicle, neighborhood garden, or do your business from home? It is now general knowledge that many successful companies, as we know them today, started from garages, bedrooms, balconies, or any other unexpected places.

Teleworking, Telecommuting or Remote working

Depending on your business's nature, Consider telecommuting/teleworking or remote working. You and your employees may not necessarily need to commute to a central area but work from your various homes or geographical locations that may or may not be outside your workplace.

Our world has gone digital, and telecommunications has played a vital role in enhanced performance.

You can decide to work with telecommunication gadgets or technologies from different locations. Work must not necessarily always be a physical or in-person convergence of people in a particular or centralized area to achieve results. Remote working and telecommuting have also produced equivalent work and more in recent times.

As far back as 2012, estimates suggest that Telecommuting or teleworking provided about 40% (about 50million) of the American job population. As a result of the coronavirus pandemic, recent estimates indicate that over 62% of Americans agree they work from home currently.

Coworking

Will you want to share space with others? Coworking is another option that is becoming very popular in many parts of the world today. Where spaces are shared with others, every person independently conducts his activity and runs his organization independently and privately.

Coworking saves cost and prevents the loneliness and isolation working alone brings. It provides collaboration and networking opportunities, Camaraderie, and friendships, while ideas and facilities are shared. Coworking can provide motivation and inspiration to succeed, especially where innovative minds share spaces.

Equipment

What type of office equipment will you need? Will you need state-of-the-art products, modern machines, and equipment, or improvise equipment for temporary use? Will you need newer software for your IT unit or vehicles to market and deliver your products? These are some of the issues you need to consider and resolve before heading out.

REGULATION:

Some organizations require either joining corporative, association, or trade unions. Also, there are state regulations, taxes, and policies guiding the registration of new business. You can enquire about this regulation, or you seek advice from a friendly Lawyer. Do not compromise on these requirements because such neglects may lead to harassments and pitfalls that may involve huge penalties that should have been avoided.

Chapter 11

START-UP ESSENTIALS

People don't have to believe in you.

For you to succeed, just work hard,

When you succeed, they will believe.

–Coach Stephen Keshi

We all need help to lift our plans and aspiration off the table. Support comes in various ways and can be primary or professional knowledge. It can be by reaching out to friends and others who are more experienced and more knowledgeable. Many are loitering and wasting away in ignorance, while others fail as a result of inexperience.

Regardless of your industry and background, help is needed in various forms of assistance. This chapter provides the required information that will guide those intending entrepreneurship.

We shall begin this chapter with a story of Abutu and a skill, not correctly channeled.

Abutu, a Chauffeur, usually sits waiting in the car while his boss is in our office. Still, that very day, Abutu followed behind Ode -the Police Orderly climbed up to the office. He greeted me and was about walking out when I offered him a seat. Probably not used to such, it took a repeated offer for him to cave in. It was lunchtime, so that I could play with time.

I have become familiar with Ode, the Orderly, and as such, we often speak freely with each other. Ode sat at the part of my office overlooking the CEO's office. That way, he'll also have an eye at his boss. It was Ode, the police orderly that started the conversation.

Ode: Sir, you know Abutu is very good with his hands

Me: Ok, not too sure where the discussion was headed

Ode: He makes excellent carports

Me: Really? As I looked in the direction of Abutu, he quietly nodded in agreement.

Me: Abutu, are you good as Ode says, I inquired, wearing a friendly smile.

Abutu: Stammers… "Sir I do my best and people often say it's the best they've seen."

Me: interesting, so how do I know you're that good? What do you offer that others rarely consider? His answers were filled with passion and regrets.

He spoke for about 3 minutes concerning his work, the finishing, material quality, and costs with some necessary elaborations.

I asked further, apart from the carport, what else he does. He mentioned security fences of all sorts and Urban thatched roofs. His knowledge of the thatched roof was terrific. He spoke about the grass quality is the best. He said most of the Abuja grass types are not durable while the best is gotten near Kaduna. He spoke at length to buttress his point.

I invited him to a window from our two-storied office overlooking another office premises. There stood a newly constructed carport though, in lay man's knowledge, I thought the job was fantastic, but Abutu took a look at it and said it was a good finishing; I nodded in agreement as he started analyzing the position. The base and the materials will not last, and the tarpaulin is not good enough because it will fade sooner; it may not survive strong wind for a long time. The iron bar that held it to the ground will rust sooner, not the best quality; it should have been larger.

I was fascinated but wondered how with so much knowledge and skill. I chose to be a chauffeur placed on a salary that resides around a minimum wage avenue.

Abutu had worked for others in his strength, skill, and productivity for about ten years receiving peanut as salary and often exploited.

Further discussion revealed so much business ignorance. Abutu has lots to offer that could bring him financial independence and stability. Unfortunately, he does not know how to exploit it, how to begin, how to positions his business. He knows nothing about starting and running a business.

Other smart business people have been using his skills to create opportunities and paying him peanut to the point he gave up on his skills and took to being a private driver.

Abutu doesn't know about business registration and corporate account. He neither knows about marketing his business nor business plan. Business proposals are foreign to him.

Abutu has a primary education, can read, write, and has the resources that are his skill and talent but lacks basic knowledge to realize his dreams. Some smart people always take advantage of such ignorance, use the skill to create wealth, employ the skill owner, and then determine the remuneration. At the same time, they are gracious for being hired. This is the summary of skilled employment! I believe a copy of a book like 'Street entrepreneurs' will change the perspective of the likes of Abutu for good forever.

CAN YOU START FULLY WHILE HOLDING YOUR JOB

It is possible to start a business while still holding your regular paid employment until, at a time, you are sure you can resign from your job and go full time into the business. This may need your hiring competent hands as you supervise and monitor your business from the side. An added advantage is that you learn the business as you hold on to your paid job. Also, you can inject additional funds from your paid job in case of financial demand or loss. This helps reduce further pressure on the owner.

It is also good to go full-blown in your new business. This gives the new business the needed attention required to run a successful start-up. In this case, you may consider making additional money available to carter for your day to day financial demand, family needs, other miscellaneous expenses, and overhead costs for at least six months.

Depending on new business for entire financial obligations, its inception often puts pressure on the business that often leads to its failure. This is part of the reason new businesses often fail. It is not always because of bad business, but it is bad business practices in such cases.

Setting aside a fund to meet the business owner's personal needs brings stability to the new business. It reduces pressure both on the business and the entrepreneur.

Going into business full-time can be challenging, especially when there is a limited fund available as often occasioned in start-ups; however, you can achieve all you set to accomplish with passion, determination, and focus.

There are other reasons to go full-blown into a business when you are fired from your job. It may provide the opportunity to sample that great idea you've been going through on your mind. Often in such time, there is a limited fund available. The positive side is that you have enough time to get absorbed into your new business.

Quality time spent working on your business can pay as many dividends in the absence of enough start-up capital as you try various ways to make up for the short cash fall. The situation could allow you to take a risk and experiment with different options available to you aimed at success. This challenge stirs you into innovations where you keep trying various ways to break even.

Being without a paid job should not be a sad moment; instead, it should provide you the opportunity to try out that idea you have been harboring instead of wallowing in self-pity.

Today lots of people are making legitimate money just with their laptops and smart phones. You may have been reading about these success stories and wonders if they are real. This may provide an opportunity to experiment with this line of business with all the time available to you. Read good business books. Google and learn an online business that you can start from home. Where necessary, you may be needed to pay a token to acquire such knowledge and skill. Some training can be learned within seven days, costing little or nothing. There is no harm in trying; you have nothing to lose if you try. You have all to gain if you are committed to the course. It could be the beginning of your success story.

Sometimes it appears the human brain function correctly and more efficiently when tasked with difficult and challenging conditions. Take advantage of the situation and task your brain into productivity.

WORKING ALONE

Often when a business opens, there are usually cash problems. There is barely enough start-up capital to run the new business. The purchasing circle varies from business to business. The process might be shorter for those into everyday household items, unlike those that manufacture or market machinery, hospital, scientific, or audiovisual equipment with a more extended purchase circle. In businesses with a longer purchase circle, upfront should be estimated and financial provision made to cover these periods.

In many cases when the business newly opens its doors, the owner may need other hands like office equipment, motor vehicle, secretary, marketers, driver, IT person, product developer, other skilled personnel and working tools but cannot often afford them as such may have to work alone providing these services personally.

These demands sometimes exceed initial expectations that could also be stressful; however, while this provides additional incentive for motivation, it also keeps the business owner busy.

The entrepreneur may often be unprepared by the weight of demand, leading the new business owner to lose focus.

In reality, while in your former paid job, you were putting up about eight to ten hours daily. Running your firm often involves doing jobs made for more than three other persons. This demands working more hours and sometimes working late into the night.

As a result of scarce resources, it is not unusual to see the new business owner at inception doing the work of the following people:
● Manager
● Secretary
● IT Man
● Business and Product Developer
● Driver, Cleaner
● Office Assistance
● Marketer
● Sales Man
● And Customer Relations Officer.

If he is fortunate to have staff, he is expected to

● Plan strategy
● Motivate staff
● Lead team
● Monitor fun
● Discover the strength and weakness of each employee
● Harness their full potentials and their limitations for growth.

If he successfully gets the desired mix, he is on his way to raising his first staff to help achieve his goals.

Of course, these all-in-one packages can keep you occupied and creative. Loneliness and boredom are a more significant challenge that can be mentally, physically, and socially draining.

It could bring discouragement, especially to those coming from an organization with colleagues, partners, and friends who share ideas and information and solve problems together.

Working alone can be tasking, challenging, and sometimes dull. Knowing that the business is your brainchild provides the overriding motivation to propel the new business owner towards achieving set goals.

There are various ways of combating loneliness and boredom when working alone—joining social network sites and platforms like Facebook, Twitter, Instagram, Linked In, Whatsapp, other professional groups, and communities that meet interest. It pays to join those forums or platforms that are related to your business.

Some of these communities provide forums for sharing ideas, making contributions, inventing new markets, and other related contributions.

Take advantage of this period listening to audio books relating to your business, listening to a radio program, watching television programs and movies that you have not done for a long time, and enhancing skill and knowledge. You may decide to explore other hobbies.

These are various ways to drive away boredom when starting up and working alone. However, there is a need to guard against being addicted to the programs instead of getting distracted and losing focus.

Working alone though demanding and tasking may help you to:

- Invent your creativity
- Develop and hone your leadership potential further

- Develop a working discipline that will help you when you eventually employ staff for your business.

COMPANY REGISTRATION

Register your company with the corporate affairs commission (CAC) or other relevant and appropriate authorities. This starts with choosing a name for your business.

While names might not determine your business's success, sometimes it is advisable to choose a name appealing to all classes of your intended clients. It is better if the name is easy to pronounce.

Your business name may be a window to the type of business you do. A business name can create bias or acceptance with a specific number of clients. Much care should be employed before deciding on a particular word.

A name may appeal to your locality or region and, as such, may attract members of your fraternity, race, or business community. At other times, the same name might have offensive meaning to different cultures or religions elsewhere.

It is valuable to use names that will most likely have universal appeal in choosing a business name. Your brand starts from your business name; therefore, it should be worthwhile getting it right at inception.

You can register as a limited liability company, public company, or business name registered to give your business a corporate image. When you register your business, it will allow you to do business with the government, other responsible and reputable organizations.

To register your business, you can walk straight into the commission's office, make an inquiry, or get advice on the proper registration type that may be suitable for your business. You can also engage the services of a lawyer and other professionals to get your company correctly registered. On registering your business with the commission, the commission will issue your certificate of incorporation. With the certificate of incorporation, your business is ready to open its doors to customers.

On opening the door to your business, it is good to separate your business from yourself even though you are the business owner. This means that you must treat the business as a person other than you. Your business need not act or behave as you as a person.

Some lifestyles may be right for you and harmful to your business survival. For example, you may feel that your status is that of a luxury car. Still, in reality, the business is not stable enough for such financial commitment. Do not use business money to fund your fun, your fantasy. This may put unnecessary pressure on the new business.

There are also times that your business will deserve an excellent corporate status to improve its corporate and brand image. Do not deny that to the business because of your conservative and straightforward lifestyle. Differences and misunderstandings can result in lawsuits; your business can be sued and taken to court by your clients, competitors, community, government, and even your staff or friends. This may arise when the activities of your business fall short of acceptable standards or norms. Practice and operate your business within the bounds of the law.

Open a Corporate \ Business Account

After registering your business\company with the corporate affairs commission (CAC), such business is now recognized as a business entity that can now stand neck to neck with any other business outfit either locally or internationally. You can now take the documents issued by the (CAC) to any bank of your choice and inquire about the type of accounts that will be suitable for your new business. The bank will educate and advise you on options that will help your business.

It is often useful to visit more than one bank and compare what they offer to help your business when needed. You may be charged a small fee to open an account, and sometimes it is free depending on the type of account you open.

You can open a savings account, but the current account will bring more value for your business purposes. The current account will bear your business name, signifying that your new business is now an entity other than you even though you are a signatory to the company's account. Examples of business account include AY. Holdings, Obyz Ventures Ltd, Arnold Nigerian Enterprise, JKM Transport, Jumaxz Integrated Services Ltd, Diamond Gold, Bronze PLC, and others.

At this stage, you can discourse with your bank manager or your account officer to know the kind of benefit or assistance in the form of financial backing and other aid that the bank can render you as your business progresses. It is good to find out these details from various banks before opening your account. This knowledge will help you decipher which of the banks that will meet your business and financial needs. This is important to your new business because you will need banks to support, if not immediately, then as your business grows.

With the Current account, your bank may consider financing your business in terms of loans and other support that may come up. Bank support is often determined by the volume of transactions, cash inflow, and outflow through your business account. It will benefit your business to allow your cash transactions to pass through your bank's current account than through your personal savings account. Corporate/company account gives your business a professional and formal outlook.

More so, not all your clients and business associates will want to pay you cash or issue cheques in your name. Most organizations prefer issuing cheque and making transfers through your company's business account rather than individual names.

Participating In Government Contracts

For new business owners who want to participate in a government's contract, various other registrations will be required to qualify for such contract bids. It varies from place to place, but these will provide a guide for your expectations.

Some of the registrations below are for professional business. Still, it may not be required of you to provide all the documents. The aim here is to help you have expectations when bidding for government and other contracts.

Below are the requirements for Government contracts:

- Your company profile indicating key staff, qualification or expertise
- Tax clearance certificate
- Evidence of registration with the CAC
- Evidence of registration with National database for contractors, consultancy and service providers
- Evidence of similar jobs executed within the past three years
- Registration with relevant professional body or institution
- Evidence of financial capability or possible bank support
- Evidence of registration with Nigeria Social Insurance Trust Fund (NSITF)
- Evidence of registration with the Bureau for Public Procurement (BPP)
- Evidence of registration and remittance with Industrial Training Fund (ITF)
- Company Audited Account for three years
- Evidence of registration with the Financial Reporting Council of Nigeria (FRC)
- Your Tin and vat number
- Evidence of compliance with the professional local content council

ASSEMBLE YOUR ARRAYS OF WORKING TOOLS:

When you start your new business, you should assemble various working tools to ease much burden off you. The tool includes some or all of the following:

- Business Card (sometimes called Complimentary card)
- Catalogue
- Introduction Letters
- Office space may be rented, shared space, your car, home, Garage, or even at a free for all neighborhood gardens.

Some of these essential tools are often neglected or ignored. Your business card must be with you at all times, as you may need to give it out to a potential client in the shortest possible time. This may be in a lift, social or corporate gatherings, and other formal and informal settings.

BUSINESS CARD

Your business card should have a simple design and not congested with information. This assists those you give them not to be confused if it's a mini-billboard, catalog, or newspaper adverts. People do not have the time to go through lots of information on a single card. It should be precise, neat, modest, and attractive. Your business card could represent the image and brand of your firm. It must not necessarily be expensive. Some information contained in your business card includes and may not be limited to the following:

- Your company name
- Logo
- Company Colour
- Slogan
- Office or industry address or location
- Telephone number
- Email address
- Company website and or Twitter handle
- Your Name and designation

While all the above elements are essential, I will take a little time to give a short explanation for these four (Name, Logo, slogan, color). This is because, like the others, they could make or mare your business.

Business Name

I discussed the importance of the business name above. It goes a little further because of its importance. Your business name could mean everything to your business. Just as when Shakespeare authored those words:

> "What's in a name?
> That which we call a rose
> By any other name
> Would smell as sweet"

Perhaps Shakespeare did not have a business outfit in our era in mind when he authored those words. The sweet-smelling rose is planted and kept in homes and family gardens in one locality for a while. It could be a resident of a cemetery in another culture. In such a culture, planting a rose made for the graveyard close to the home may be interpreted as a bad omen. Yet the same rose is adored and used to beautify homes in another culture.

Business name matters a lot these days because of the political climate, religion, culture, demographic and geographical factors playing roles in how a business name may be accepted locally, nationally, and globally.

A particular name with religious connotation may influence its marketing acceptability in one pastoral setting. It may have another meaning in another culture. This can course sales problems in that environment.

I remember back in secondary school, especially the day a new student joined our class. His name sounded right until it was written on the chalkboard, and the whole class erupted in a feast of laughter. This chaos almost overwhelmed the class teacher.

The name 'Otuka' meaning 'one is greater' or 'one is mightier' but when written on the blackboard could also be pronounced 'female sex organ is greater or female sex organ is mightier' in another dialect. Also, in another same dialect name, 'otuka' means 'same discussion.' Here is a word with exact spelling but three different pronunciations and three different meanings!

You can only imagine how that name (if a business name) will be accepted in some quarters where you may not be available to give your pronunciation and meaning.

Your business name should be simple to pronounce, easy to remember and as much as possible strive to cut across cultures, religion, geographical and demographical setting.

Again some names are tailored to a specific business line and may not accommodate other businesses should you want to introduce new products in the future. For example, Chris Foods And Confectionaries will not be good enough should you wish to add the manufacture of electric cables to your line of business. Therefore, it becomes imperative that, depending on your business and plans, choose a name that will accommodate the expansion and introduction of other products that may not be part of the business's original line.

However, unless you are in a specialized business, the name can reflect such a particular business line. Your business name could add to the marketability of your product.

Logo

If you think your logo is unique and special, safeguard it by getting a trademark for it. This is to forestall another using and taking over such a logo. As in your business name, your logo should cut across divides, especially in this era of globalization.

Slogan

Keep your slogan short, simple, and to the point. Your slogan can convey your products or company's unique message.

Colour

We know that color conveys different messages, but a well-built house may lose all efforts and brilliance in its construction due to the wrong choice of colors. At other times, a home that is not all that fantastic can become classy due to the right mix of colors. During weddings, you notice the bride and groom choosing colors that may reflect their personality and the personality of their love. Your business color, even in its aesthetics, has to reflect the nature of your business.

CATALOG

Your business may need a catalog that can be distributed to your customers or as a handout. This provides another means of advertising your business.

The catalog contains pictures and images of your company products.

Your customers should determine what business you are into by taking a look at your catalog. Also, the record contains the company name, location, and other related contact information.

Catalogs are often made colorfully attractive and pleasant to the eyes. This is aimed to catch the attention of prospective clients. The catalog provides a more comfortable and cheaper medium to advertise your product.

You can package your catalog, your company's introduction letter, your business card, and mail them to potential clients. It can be handed out to clients or placed in strategic places, where targeted customers, visitors, and guests can quickly scan through them or pick them.

Your catalog can get to places you never imagined, with your email address, phone number, and website included in it. You may get surprise calls or emails from places your catalogs have reached.

You may solicit a professional's help to design and produce a neat catalog that may attract and generate sales for your new company.

Catalogs are beneficial to the business; you can still receive a response from those you sent them to, years after you had sent it.

Chapter 12

BODY SERVICING

Business demands fitness for peak productivity and success. The body's well-being adds to the success of your business. With demand needed in our rat race business environment, sometimes moving from one domain to another can be very taxing and demanding. Below are health tips for optimum performances needed to consider before opening your business door. This chapter started with Amala's story, the energetic business magnate who placed his priority where he thought mattered.

Amala is a friend of my Dad spanning over three decades. He is a good and generous businessman. It is a very detailed man with sharp, bright, restless eyes. This eye is also keen on spotting opportunities months or years before others see it. He travels a lot on a business trip across the country and overseas. He is picky in his airline choice, and he flies with the top 3 airlines known for their safety standards. He postpones any deal if these three airlines are fully booked. His cars are always in mint condition and often serviced even before the due date. But there's a caveat! Amala rarely pays as much attention to his own body.

On the contrary, he'll postpone the doctor's appointment for the next business meeting. He jokes about it that he will not die till his dying day or that something must eventually kill a man as he laughed heartily.

He drinks and smokes with a devil's care attitude, being the vice he loves. His friends often playfully call him chimney or brewery, but you can't get him drunk. -Chimney because of his smoking habit and brewery as a result of heavy drinking.

The years have passed, and the body had caved in to assault unleashed overtime. He had been on different health issues.

Lifestyle changes are medically prescribed and strictly followed. He is a wealthy man and has the money but poor health that won't even allow for mere painless leisure or vacations.

HEALTH

It is said that health is wealth and rightly said, you will need to keep ahead of the market, the competition, and keep the customer happy. Meetings, travel, following leads, observing market forces yet abreast with day to running of the business are part of the demand that success entails.

These demand attention to health. Health here refers to the conditions of the physical, mental, or spiritual well-being. Often, we do not value our health or prioritize until we lose it or like Amala. We are trapped in chronic health challenges and have to life-changing decisions that alter our lives due to health problems.

The World Health Organization (WHO) defines health as a state of complete physical, mental, and social well-being, not merely the absence of disease or infirmity.

Business owners need to personalize the World health organization (WHO) definition of health to their advantage and their business's success.

In the past decades, foods consisted of more vegetables and less junk food. It can be discovered that with inadequate medical facilities in many areas across the globe back then, the people of that era seemed to have lived a relative amount of longer life than its seen today, even with the advancement in health system delivery and wonder drugs. They go to bed after a trying day and enjoy a healthy dose of night rest.

Today, in our modern, fast-paced generation, we chase businesses and contracts, beat deadlines, close deals, meet targets, get an education and more education, and train and retrain. We travel from state to state, countries, across continents, and have also conquered outer space. We have little or no time for deserved rest. We postpone retirement, doctors' appointments, and even vacation in pursuit of wealth.

Eventually, we lose our health while chasing wealth and, if lucky to be alive, live the remaining years of our life in agony and reminiscence of what we should have done better, especially about our health.

The old nursery rhyme reminds us that early to bed early to rise makes a man healthy, wealthy, and bright! Agreed that in our modern era, there is more money needed to pay bills; purchase domestic gas, fuel cars, pay for waste disposals, recharge our phones, pay the water bill, electricity bill, internet and cable network bills, pay rents, car park, mortgages, school fees and tuition, security bills, local government bills, metro bills, insurance bills, other taxes, and endless utilities. Therefore an early-to-bed rhyme leaves a man poor and broken. Amidst this double jeopardy, there is the need to underscore the benefit of the much-needed rest and attention to health.

Medical experts advise that we need a minimum of eight hours of sleep each day and eight cups of water per day to function well and live healthy, productive lives.

Today we take bites, tea, coffee, and snack-on with experience. We junk up our stomachs hastily and intermittently as we dive from one business meeting, conference, seminar, workshop, zoom meetings, and podcast as we close mega deals.

To curb these life-threatening feeding habits that erode our internal organs, it brings death in slow motion or spontaneously. Nutritionists have called for a 'U' turn in our eating habits. Reverting to the old order of larger balanced meals for breakfast has been suggested to enhance productivity and healthier life.

Moderate meals in the afternoon and little or no food at dinner are canvassed and campaigned. Some nutrition experts have advised a complete meal of fruits or vegetables during supper.

In the morning, the cache eats like a king; in the afternoon, eat like a prince and eat like a pauper in the evening.

Here, advocates are going back to our great grandparents' order with natural intelligence as they ate their meals, Civilization now in reverse!

We stand in puzzles while with our advancement in medicine and more knowledge about the causes of various ailments, we still battle with the scourge of cancer, high blood pressure, tumor, diabetes, venereal diseases, acquired immune deficiency syndrome, and lately the arrival of the much-anticipated virus pandemic also known as the Coronavirus or Covid-19. Our eating habits, lifestyles, and environmental factors are arguably the prime suspects contributing to this up shoot of common health challenges and deaths.

One is confounded how the human body continually withstands different kinds of abuse and assault it receives each day. That we often seem in awe when the body packs up and infests with a surge in health challenges can be the height of ignorance.

When you use low or threatening engine oil regularly or consistently in your automobile engine, you most certainly be punished with an inadequate, unreliable, and disappointing performance. In less than no time, you will be wondering why your car has finally packed up while those of your colleagues purchased the same time with yours are still in excellent mint condition. The answer is not far fetched; they take care of their automobiles. They also service and run maintenance when due, use quality engine oil and hydraulic.

Owners of a private jet, airline operators, and others who are always on the roads or air have learned one thing out of hindsight and follow it religiously for optimum performance and safety; they service these machines when due. They engage the best servicing maintenance companies and use recognized durable quality spare parts. They spare no cost to keep these machines in top shape and condition.

But here's the irony of it all. Most of these individuals who commit large funds to keep machines in mint condition often pay less attention to their health. Like Amala, they usually pay dearly not through the devices but their own weakened and unattended body.

Let us imagine what happens to the human mind and body when gulped with alcohol -beer, rum, gin, or smoke up the body daily with a cigarette or other hard drugs. Others enjoy red meat plates and other unimaginable animals for meat, sometimes eaten raw or half-cooked. Some of these animals are hosts to various pathogens! Junk foods, diet sodas, energy drinks, and chemical juice produced to last longer by preservatives, additives in juice, and other beverages with loads of white sugar into the body has become the new normal.

After closing the day, catching fun, relaxing with unprotected sex, and sometimes with multiple sex partners! The body is loaded with different life-threatening health challenges and numerous accumulations of sexually transmitted diseases!

As if such abuses are not enough, some ladies after doses of unprotected sex are left to deteriorate their bodies with frequent abortions further while others are on regular daily doses of other pills.

The anus originally and exclusively made to evacuate the body's gases and solid waste is not spared of this abuse. It has also been made an instrument of anal sex!

The way humanity is going in the craze for sexual gratification is becoming alarming. One may not be surprised if every hole in the human body, including the ears and the noses, will not someday be surgically converted to sexual instruments.

In an era of unbridled mentorship, celebrities, music idols, and other sports stars have set the stage in defining beauty and morality.

The lips are blown up to be fuller, so are the breasts pumped and popped up with silicon and other enlargements inducing chemicals. The hips and butts are injected to be fuller. Sometimes, these enlargements collapse or rupture unexpectedly and get the body acting like a car needing an alignment.

The faces are so tightened to remove wrinkles and look younger that sometimes they seem to lose every facial expression and, at other times, could be shapeless.

The skin is not left out in these abuses. They are either toned or bleached out of natural order. They have often tattooed out of vitality that sometimes the skin ends up looking like graffiti.

Oral Piercings sometimes leave the lips and the entire body open to infections, allergic reactions and, at other times, expose one to nervous damages in the tongue and gum.

The hairs, nails, teeth, eyes, or sex organs are now changed at will. Mr. James today can become Miss Jennifer the next time we meet while Miss Sandra today can turn Mr. Sanders by her next birthday. In the course of all this, the body degenerates to suffer self-inflicted afflictions.

For the aspiring entrepreneur, good health will be an advantage. A healthy body is often an outcome of personal discipline and a healthy lifestyle. Healthy lifestyles are a necessity. It involves moderate use of good and withdrawal, abstinence, and reduced harmful lifestyles like smoking, alcohol, coffee, soda, junk food, sugary products, and unprotected sex.

It will take a healthy mind to give a beneficial judgment, make a healthy decision, and work efficiently to reach set goals.

MAINTAIN IDEAL WEIGHT

A simple lifestyle adjustment can prevent many deadly diseases we grapple with in todays' world. There is an urgent need to watch what we put in our mouth and, by extension, our body and mind. There is an urgent need to pay attention to what goes into our body as we enjoy ourselves and catch fun because, at a later time, they will either hunt or benefit us.

Consider these seven commonsense health habits as espoused by Herbert. E. Douglas:

- Don't smoke
- Use little or no alcohol
- Start the day with a good breakfast
- Avoid eating in-between meals (*or eat fruits or vegetables instead*)[16]
- Sleep seven to eight hours each night
- Engage in frequent and regular exercise[17]

Douglas went on to say that nonsmokers can enjoy risk factors 80% less than their smoking friends, a much lower rate of death from mouth, throat, and bladder cancer. Nonsmokers have a significantly reduced danger of getting a terrible disability called emphysema, in which every breath becomes hard work.

Non-smokers will enjoy much better physical endurance and night vision, lower heart disease risk, and avoidance of Reynaud's disease.

Also, smoking causes what has come to be referred to as smokers' faces, characteristics that make smokers look older than their age.

---

[16] words in italics mine

[17] HOW TO SURVIVE IN THE 21ST CENTURY -Herbert .E. Douglas)

Cigarette smokes contain over four thousand toxins, most of which are absorbed directly into the skin. This smoke causes the skin to thin due to poor circulation; such makes lines and marks more noticeably hence the reasons for wrinkles around the mouth and eyes, often deep lines in smokers' cheeks.

Other characteristic includes pale and grey skin. Smoking also causes the blood vessels in the top layer of the skin to constrict, reducing the amount of oxygen in the blood, causing sickly pallor. Smoking cause's reduction in the production of collagen needed to keep skin plump and firm.[18]

Alcohol, on its part, impairs judgment.

Running a start-up needs best judgment and decision by making the right decision that contributes to its continuous growth.

WATER

Water is necessary for normal body functioning. The health benefit of taking adequate water is becoming general knowledge. However, the crux of the matter is that while many know these benefits, taking sufficient water could be a challenge—not being consistent or not taking it seriously. The average adult human body is 50- 65% water.

The percentage of water in infants is much higher, typically around 75-78% water, but dropping to 65% by one year of age. Body water composition varies according to gender and fitness level because fatty tissue contains less water than lean tissue.

The average adult male is about 60% water. The average adult woman is about 55% water because women naturally have more fatty tissue than men. The amount of water in the human body ranges from 50 to 75%, although, on average, the body is about 50 to 65% water[19]

---

[18] www.sparkpeople.com

The brain and heart are composed of 73% water.
The lungs are about 83% water.
The skin contains 64% water.
The muscles and kidneys are 79%
And even the bone is watery, 31% water![20]

Water keeps us in good health by flushing toxins out of our system and vital organs. Simultaneously, the carbohydrates and proteins that our body uses as food are metabolized and transported by water to our bloodstream.

Water lubricates our joints and transport nutrients to the cells. It keeps our throat, nose, ear, and tissue adequately moist. It regulates our internal body temperature through sweating and perspiration. Water acts as a shock absorber to the fetus, brain, and spinal cord.

When we lack water in our bodies, we feel tired and sapped of energy. This is usually called dehydration. Our body also loses water through different body activities like bowel movements. Water can also be lost through breath, vomiting, urine, and sweat.

Body water can be replenished by drinking clean, pure water and eating foods containing water examples: beverages, fruits, and vegetables.

An adequate amount of water to be taken each day cold varies due to environmental factors and job nature.

People in the Tropics are expectedly inclined to take much more water than those in temperate regions.

People who do more physical tasking work lose more water than those in offices with reduced body movement. Experts recommend at least eight cups of water each day (about 1.9 liters). The institute of medicine recommends AI (adequate Intake) for men about 3

[19] educationchemistry. about.com

[20] H.H Mitchell, Journal of Biological Chemistry

liters (13cups) each day while AI for women is 2.2 liters, about 9 cups per day. Keep in mind the general axiom; Water is Life!

Chapter 13
UTILITY PLAYER AND SELF-DEVELOPMENT
Be the best in what you do
But do not forget that
How you talk, what you say,
How you dress and how you move
Tell more of who you are
-Carnegie.

Sometimes, our skills and qualifications are not enough to reach our desired height. As such, we often need a utility player's versatility and competence to deliver on our goals. Such versatility will be gained by additional self-development.

Being a utility player doesn't make one jack-of-all-trade. If it does, then you're master of all because it recognizes your versatility.

Versatile players are often referred to as utility players because they provide team options and more advantages.

A utility player is one that can play in several positions competently. It is commonly used in sports like football, baseball, rugby, volleyball, and water polo.

A utility player is a manager's delight as it brings additional options and dependability to the team.

A utility player can play in the center's wings, backline, and even as forward in football. Although they can play well in several positions, utility players may have their default positions where they prefer or function far better. Though utility players often make the team selection, they are usually inclined to start from the bench. Yet they hold out various positions competently!

Self-development is a deliberate attempt at working on oneself to be a utility player. The aim is to have the versatility of proficiency that increases your value to blend in manners that ensure vertical and horizontal growth.

This increase in value starts with you as an individual. Self-development ensures personal progress, a progress that begins from within.

It is self-evident, an enhancement of your qualities, a polished demeanor.

It is a refinement in attitude, manner, conduct, performance, appearance, behavior, character, comportment, bearing, assertiveness, and outlook. The progress, so witness starts from deliberate intention to improve one's general personal view. These are the gains of self-development.

Self-Development Tips For Success.

A candle is worthless until it is taken out of the shelves and gives light as it turns out, for that is the purpose of its maker. There is a constant need for personal improvement.

Humans are like the candle packaged and loaded with the necessary potential to shine. Man is of less worth when he fails to utilize his possibilities to develop values, create opportunities, and achieve his innermost imagination and objectives.

With the right knowledge, man can be better in what he does now, better than who he is presently, and can acquire that personality he admires in others yet be original in his ways.

There is no argument against being conservative or traditional in your ways and approaches. Still, an ounce of personal refinement adds to a better individual.

Things must not necessarily be done when they were handed to you from your ancestors. Even DNA's are being altered or improved in this era.

Your lineage was the best herbalist known for their effective herbal medicine and perhaps lived in the bush as an herbalist. You can produce the same herbal medicine under the most hygienic condition, with exquisite packaging and modern equipment.

You can bring better packaging to that product and adequately introduce it to the market in ways that meet global standards.

Your father was known to be brash, very loud, and compulsive in his work environment and social circle but was tolerated back then. Are you sure you will still be tolerated in these times in your social process, even when you feel it's in your genetic makeup? Today, be rest assured that you will be avoided in your circle or workplace as if you are a plague. You can learn to change such a poisonous trait.

Your mother is known to have the fastest speed on a typewriter keyboard, hitting 218 words per minute with no error. You can upgrade to computer apps proficiency or be prepared to watch yourself in perpetual wants and lack.

Your uncles, third cousins, the relatives before them where bicycle repairers of note, and you have decided to toe that line. Ask yourself, how many people ride a bicycle in your neighborhood, or are you ready to talk people into a bicycle renaissance as a means of mobility. Are you still following a dying profession?

The need to continually seek personal improvement makes for a better individual. These include improvement in mannerism, etiquette, communication, dressing, table manner, skills, carriage, and managing finances. These may put you in pole position for a better you. They will accelerate the achievement of your goals and objectives in life's endeavors.

You can make yourself better than who you are at the moment. In this era of an upgrade, man can also choose to upgrade himself!

Over the years, I have observed that etiquette, carriage, mannerism, style, and clear communication seem to be one distinguishing difference between the poor and the rich, the high and mighty.

The above knowledge probably makes the rich and famous stand out in the crowd and perhaps part of why they send their children to the best schools to keep on improving in style.

Fortunately, without copying, everyone can acquire these attributes and socialize effectively with every class of people without inferiority to other global citizens.

Improving your personality will add flavor to your life. This can be achieved by observing those who are better than you in specific areas. Visit first-class hotels, seminars, or conferences that attract influential and highly distinguished individuals, especially in your interest area. Relate or observe the educated, skilled, and royals noting their carriage, etiquette, and demeanor.

Alternatively, you can enroll in improvement programs and masterclasses. You can develop your hobbies and read good books to help you achieve your aim and fine-tune your capabilities.

In this digital age, where we are online daily, the internet is piled and inundated with knowledge and information. It is now said that information is the new currency of the globe. Information and knowledge that can be gotten almost for free can surf the net at your leisure to seek various ways for self-improvement.

You can acquire primary education at home via a private tutor or online programs; knowledge gained will go a long way to enhance efficiency.

Improvement should be a lifelong plan and process. The day you lose the will to improve, you begin to retrogress and degenerate.

Improvement does not necessarily imply copying others because copying could make one fake, losing your uniqueness and the essence of who you are.

Self-development is multifaceted activities that eventually improve personal value. Personal development can be tailored to meet individual needs.

Below are a few primary areas of development to start with.

Personal Branding
Personal branding encompasses how you see yourself, your assessment, confidence, and self-worth. Self-worth should not necessarily be viewed under the prism of currency value. It contains your dignity, pride, self-esteem, and a positive outlook.

Personal branding, also called personal packaging, has to do with how you see yourself. It is about your carriage, style, or etiquette. It stems from your inner confidence, your self-confidence!

Self-confidence arises as a business person because you know your products and sure of its efficacy and values. You know for sure the satisfaction that potential clients will receive from using your products.

Personal branding can influence a positive outcome on how people perceive, value, and treat you.

When adequately conducted, it could gain you and your organization's attention among your competitors and clients. Personal branding will bring about an increase in your products' market share and gain genuine recognition and promotion.

As a startup, there is a need to market yourself before you sell your product. That is, to make yourself accessible, presentable, and refined enough, so your personality will bring respect also to your work. As the product gains market prominence, it is natural that you will no longer be visible, but your product takes center stage. When this is achieved, then you know you are making business progress.

At the inception of a business, you are the front line of your business, your product's visual image, the origin, and your brand's extension.

Your presentation, carriage, and knowledge of your products will rub-off on your goods and services in view of the above. This means that your personality will substantially impact your success at inception because you are part of your business brand.

Wikipedia, the free encyclopedia, defines Personal Branding or Packaging as the Creation of an asset that pertains to a particular person or individual. This includes but is not limited to the body, clothing, appearance, and knowledge within, leading to an indelible impression of the essence of who you are that is uniquely distinguishable.

.

Self-confidence

Self-confidence grows when you are sure of your ideas and knows your products in and out, having a firm conviction and passion for what you are doing. You cannot have self-confidence when you do not trust yourself and your ideas and have no passion for what you are doing. Your products' confidence is hinged on the strength of excellence of your knowledge. This translates to a positive outlook on your part.

Such confidence arises from a firm conviction on the efficacy of your idea or product. Confidence feeds the ability to come out with your head held high after every challenge, no matter the outcome. It is the tenacity to keep trying to unlock one's potential despite disappointment and failure.

I met Mike during a national assignment, a fellow that gets along quickly with everyone. Mike handles difficult tasks in ways that leave colleagues within the bother of envy and admiration. Complex tasks are accomplished in ways that seem so easy. He has confidence you can adore, covet, or hate.

How Mike got his dream job is seen in the ease with which he discharged duties that came his way. There was an interview for three vacancies at one of the prominent organizations. Mike arrived uninvited yet late. His packaging made the people at customer service to grant him attention and access. Soon he was headed to the branch controller's office as if a client needs to see the controller. Of course, he was allowed in; the latter got the job way ahead of others who had already been considered.

Months later, I asked to know how he did it. Mike told me that when he entered the branch controller's office and was offered a seat, in seconds, he looked around and notice different golf pictures and trophies on the wall and office chest. Those pictures and awards were the ice breaker that started the conversation on golf as the controller; a seasoned and passionate golfer took time to show his winnings at different times and places. It appeared the controller just realized that he was talking to a stranger, an unknown guest!

By the time they got down to business, and the controller realized he has been speaking with a job-seeking candidate on a mission to secure a job in an institution he cherished. The controller had mixed feelings of love-hate, surprise, and respect towards the job seeker.

Mikes' confidence and natural intelligence had warmed him to the heart of the controller! Later the controller personally sent an endorsement note to his team, which may have aided in getting the job, which he never applied for in an era of protocol and sea of job seekers!

To gain self-confidence, there is a need to modify values and make decisions based on conviction and strength of quality ideas, invariably acting according to what you think to be your best choice, but not feeling too bad when your choices did not yield much as you expected.

SELF DEVELOPMENT: EDUCATION

Education is essential in today's world. Primary education to read and write is obligatory. To the business owner, it should be seen as a prerequisite to starting. There is no age barrier in improving oneself both in academic education and in your occupational training.

No matter what you do, where you live, and who you are, education will add value and progress to your chosen career.

Whatever your profession, occupation, nomad, craftsman, or trading, primary education will make success easier to achieve.

Get educated in your area of interest; this may mean going beyond your academics to acquiring occupational skill and expertise.

This may involve acquiring education in your crafts, arts, or vocation, but first, in whatever type of education, strive to get a necessary academic foundation. Basic education help's one function efficiently and effectively in today's world.

The world is getting small, where boundaries rarely exist. In Globalization, we see an interconnected world, an unimaginable increased free trade of goods and services, where access to technology has removed borders and restrictions.

Communication now happens through various media platforms, making exchanges easier and effective. The internet ushers in a world that is akin to town square meetings. Today we have platforms of unimaginable human interaction where various discussions and activities are treated by participants across the global defeating time difference and multicultural differences.

You can be at your dining table, in the comfort of your car, or your ranch and traverse the entire world while transacting multimillion-dollar business. All that is needed to achieve this excellent fit is mere primary education that allows you access to very affordable smart technologies. Please take advantage of the opportunities available to prepare and be part of a fast-moving train of street entrepreneurs poised to get it right through innovations.

In addition to your primary education, train, retrain, go ahead and prepare yourself. Get skill, obtain the gift, acquire talent, gain, and attain mastery and skills. Skill and primary education are the meat of the matter.

If you can, get your diploma, degree, postgraduate degrees, Ph.D., by all means, do so and just get qualified.

Always be prepared; the opportunity will come knocking someday. The worst day of your life is the day that a tremendous out-of-the-box opportunity comes knocking at your door. You realize you are unqualified to grab the chance, especially when it dawns on you that you had had all the time to have gotten prepared.

There is always something unique in every one of us. Education will help identify, master, and make the best of your potentials. Skill will bring excellence to who you are and what you do.

Do not underrate skill acquisition and do not overrate academic qualification; both harmoniously merged bring in a confluence of excellence, waking the genius in you.

SELF-DEVELOPMENT: COMMUNICATION
Communication involves speaking, listening, writing, gestures, facial expression, body language, and feedback.

For effective communication to take place, there must be clarity at all times. Strive to be clearly understood by your audience, team, or partner.

Do not assume you are understood or that they ought to understand by your body language or previous experiences. Be sure you are understood by communicating clearly.

You aim to get work done, make decisions, achieve set goals, get feedback, develop relationships, and enrich your social capital. This can be achieved by acquiring the ability to interact and communicate effectively with others in any given situation.

Communication is essential even to animals as well. In their habitats, animals understand the power of touch. Sometimes communication serves as a defense mechanism to fight or flight from predators. Wrongly applied, communication by one animal at the wrong time can lead to the death of other animals. This we have often watched in Nat Geo Wild.

The hunter's tale of folklore could illustrate this. A fable had it that two bush fowls were perched on low tree close-by singing like nightingales on a particular day. The snake coiled close to the tree beneath the birds, called out to the birds, and advised they should try and keep quiet as this will attract the hunter who will shoot down one or both birds. The noise of the gunshot will disorganize other animals far and near in the forest. On picking up the bird, the hunter will notice the snake coiled under the grass; the hunter will kill the snake and, in the process, cut the grass. He will also cut a tree branch with which the hunter will carry the snake.

So, one sweet communication at the wrong time will not just affect the birds involved but other animals, plants, and the entire ecosystem.

This is a classic example of how one wrong communication can affect the entire system. Information wrongly communicated can send an entire army on military action against another nation.

An old school mate will always be shaking his head in disagreement while you're speaking once your position in an argument or discussion runs contrary to his opinion or views. He does that even without saying a word. This attitude is often offensive and often leads to heated exchanges that live either or both hurting after a discussion.

There is a need to recognize that others are passionate about their opinions. Their opinions must be respected even when such views are not as sound as expected; the person must be allowed to air that opinion. Instead of making their argument look inferior, you can find ways to bring them to your point of view without hurting their ego. This way, either when they win or lose the argument, you gain a friend.

Sometimes, people mistake chatterbox, fast-talking, and quick-talking as been natural communicators. Each of these talkers is just what they are called, talkers! They do not communicate! They rarely pay attention to another persons' viewpoint. Still, They are more interested in what they want to say next even as their discussants speak.

Sometimes it appears such people are in love with the sound of their voice as such another person's agent does not appeal to them. They always seem to believe their own opinion to be more superior to that of their opponents. They find it funny to put others down while expressing their views. These sorts of people pay little or no attention. In contrast, others make contributions but want everyone else to pay attention when they speak.

You don't need to be an orator to communicate effectively. You can as well communicate efficiently and effectively without speaking much. Effective communication can be achieved even in silence. Communication can be achieved without altering a word but listening attentively to what another is saying. It could also be attained by body language or even facial expression at the right time.

Of course, people are naturally gifted in communicating effectively, yet such people can also improve their communication skills.

Effective communication is an art that can be acquired or learned. You can learn to be an excellent public speaker just as you can learn to improve your interpersonal communication skill.

To be effective in communication, respect another person's viewpoint even when it appears they are not making the expected intelligent contributions. It might interest you to know that they are also passionate and convinced about their views. You will gain nothing by damaging their self-esteem if you respond to them negatively. Instead, by paying attention and gentle correction, you inadvertently show respect to their expression and turn them to your superior views without deflecting their ego. This way, you gain a friend who respects your opinion and know you also show him respect. This then is an outcome of effective communication.

Self-Development: Managing finances
Without a grip on your finances, your success will be delayed as debts mount. My grandfather used to say that once the mentally poor get their first big money, they begin to imagine that the source will continue to flow. With the new quid in hand, their plan goes viral in tens of places, of things to buy but far from investing.

Unfortunately, most of these plans and ideas will not include options and plans to create further wealth. Reinvestment is usually out of the equation. Luxury that is not needed at the moment becomes a priority. He will first acquire those things that will not earn him more income.

Consideration of those things that he desires that have eluded him for a long dulls logical reasoning. It becomes about the acquisition of Luxury cars, jewelry, designer clothing, the newest version of the tablet, the latest flat screen and home theatre, Italian furniture, and other modern gadgets that become obsessed with such minds.

All at once, if the money can carry it, he announces his arrival to wealth by his attitude and lifestyle, not minding that a newer version of the gadgets may be released in less than no time. Shortly he realizes that the source is not yielding as expected.

The first business breakthrough should be reinvested to strengthen and consolidate the business. Unfortunately, it will be used to acquire luxuries that could have been delayed or deferred.

I have often heard some people say, "if things did not work out as planned then they have to sell them back." Sell them back?

This could only mean that they know they are not yet ripe for that kind of expenditure. Regrettably, such luxuries have little or no second-hand value and, as such, will not meet the expenses that should have been avoided with careful financial discipline. This is the tale of the lowest financial minded fellows. It's a tale that has been told and retold, yet most young people often get themselves short at the feet.

It will be difficult for a spendthrift to run a business successfully, especially at the early stage. Wealth cannot grow by wastage and reckless spending.

Wealth is created by the wise and prudent investment, sacrifice, strategic planning, and the ability to invest today and reinvest profits while you wait.

If you desire to be successful, identify a career, a skill, and then invest in that skill or profession. Then learn to use that acquisition to serve society, get paid, and don't be extravagant with the proceeding.

Learn to patiently grow gradually by deferring gratification and reduce or forgo avoidable expenses. Finally, success shows up while on it.

As you grow your business, remember, good things are never exhausted. Money, luxury, or wealth does not 'run away' forever, and materialism outlives the man. You can acquire those wants tomorrow while you invest today.

The haste for materialism sometimes causes business owners to fall into avoidable pitfalls that cause business failure.

You have the option of growing your business where you can easily purchase not just your needs but your wants without causing an upset to the business.

Deferred gratification, also called delayed gratification, would make the difference between successful and unsuccessful people.

This involves letting go of your short-term desires for a long-term benefit. This is the foundation of success.

Financial discipline is essential to a new business owner as it ensures progress and erases unnecessary debts.

Self-development: Masterclass

Masterclasses are online digital learning platforms or online classes from experts, instructors, and professionals in various skills or fields. They help you master a particular skill of your choice. This is done online using a computer or phone as you learn from the comfort of your home. The masterclass is through audio or video presentations, often through the channel of electronic mail.

Interested individuals make payment to the instructor as the sign up for the masterclass. You can learn photography, business skill, gym, writing skills, dance, music, painting arts and craft, digital marketing, cake making, confectionaries, and other skills through these master instructors and professionals.

You may have seen it all over the internet without paying attention to them, don't keep brushing it aside. You identified that anyone that meets your interest would add value to your career, business, or vocation. Often they are very affordable and may even have the opportunity for free trials. The masterclass will bring new knowledge and skills to you in the comfort of your home and at your own time.

Part 3
EYES ON THE PRICE! IT'S ALL ABOUT YOU:

Chapter 14
PROFICIENCY AND PASSION

Passion and knowledge of new business

My friend, Paul, runs a successful Landscaping and interior decoration outfit. I remember back in early 2000 when his company opened a business. He worked hard for years to get the best out of his business, but a breakthrough wasn't immediate in sight.

The persistence, commitment, and doggedness in his effort were terrific as he nurtured his business unrelentingly.

On more than one occasion, when the business eventually picked up new government regulations within the Federal Capital Territory threatened confiscation or demolition with no compensations for his investments. He had earlier written and gotten approval from the authorities to develop and manage the garden for a specific number of years.

When his garden, 'The Urban Villager,' was taken away by federal might, which would have marked an end to most business owners but not Paul.

After a series of frustration by the authorities, Paul discovers an inner will, strength, and drives to start all over. Not just starting over halfheartedly but starting over with renewed zeal and new knowledge. He kept improving and learning better ways of doing things and introducing new products to his original idea.

For seven years, his business was on slow growth, but Paul was not the type to quit on what he set his mind to accomplish. His breakthrough came about the seventh year in the business.

By his action, Paul defied and rewrote statistics that 'most business fail within the first Five years' to 'most businesses can still pick up big-time after the first seven years.'

Today his company manages the many prominent organizations and Government establishments in the Federal Capital and other states, thereby creating employment for many young promising unskilled, skilled, and other professionals! It was a battle for relevance long fought.

His organization has introduced innovations in landscaping and interior décor businesses that have caught individuals' attention and small and large organizations.

When we met not too long ago, I was amazed at the rate at which his company has grown. I asked Paul how he was able to continue for years after each disappointment.

His three-word answers were **Passion**, **Resilience**, and **Never Despairing**.

Paul kept on because he had a passion for landscaping, such as he would have done it with little or no remuneration. He chose not to do it part-time so that he can give it his best shot.

When you hear him speak about his business, you see the passion radiating on his face and listen to it flow from his heart through his voice.

His success story shows that it will be difficult to defeat a person who is unwilling to give up on a conviction or idea! Those three words (Passion, Resilience, and Never Despairing) are the hallmarks of Paul's triumph.

Resilience is the will to go on after each failure and disappointment because you have tremendous confidence in your idea; it comes from passion. You become like the elastic after each stretching; you rebound and move on. Great confidence in your ideas plus passion produces resilience.

Paul was once a Street Entrepreneur; today, his business has joined the big league front line and admired metropolitan companies and success stories hewed from the street to the boardrooms through constant innovation.

Entrepreneurs are often passionate about what they are about to go into, resilient in pursuing that great idea or goal, and never despair.

Make out time to learn about that new business you plan to go into, even if you are to employ professionals as members of staff. Poor knowledge creates unnecessary problems.

The street entrepreneur must continue to upgrade in the business's knowledge, for therein lies the real and sustainable success.

Make haste slowly when venturing into new business. Do not allow the passion, excitement, and appeal to drive you to a hasty decision.

Growing up as a child in my neighborhood, there used to be a saying that 'any rodent that forgets to cover his exit as he goes out, may return to find a snake will use reverse to escape from its hole. That is if the rodent made it out alive. So are businesses hastily set up without required skills, knowledge, or modalities to provide training or learning while in the business. More so, you can collaborate or partner with someone that can provide the experience you need to run a successful business.
Never despair!
Life situations will throw challenges at you and, at times, with no headway insight. Always remember that somewhere in that situation lies the way of escape to victory. Never despair!

In his book, How to develop self-confidence and influence people by public speaking, Dale Carnegie gave Marshal Foch the story of who led to victory, one of the greatest armies the world has ever seen. "Marshal Foch declared that he had only one virtue; Never Despairing.

When the French had retreated to Maine in 1914, General Joffre instructed the Generals under him in charge of two million men to stop fleeing and begin an offensive. This new battle, one of the most decisive in the history of the world, has raged for two days. When General Foch, in command of Joffre's Centre, sent him one of the most impressive messages in Military records, 'My Centre gives way, my rights recede, the situation is excellent, I shall attack.'
That attack saved Paris".

The tiger that strays into the village fights his way out in escape and survival. The villagers misinterpret it as an act of courage and created folklore on the tiger's escapade and bravery. He dared to enter the village and fight his way out.

So when the fight seems most challenging, and the Centre of your life seems to recede, don't give up. Still, like General Foch or a tiger, that can provide an ideal situation. Attack, attack, attack, and fight your way out. After all, when you are at the bottom, there is only one way to go up, up, up!

Business Behaviors

"The Horse was King, and almost everything grew around him.
Then, to the scream Of the Horse, the change began.
The brass –lamped motor car came coughing up the road."
-Laurie Lee

The business environments are full of unexpected changes. It could be disruptive innovations, change in government policies, budgets, shifts in the economy's direction, or change in trend, tastes, fashion styles, and cultural differences. It may be a drift toward the consumption of luxury items, foreign goods, or demographic changes. These changes can impact the business environment.

With the arrival of the information era, of which the younger generation often determines the trend. Social media has provided a platform that could trigger spontaneous and unexpected change within the shortest time. We are now a generation flooded with information!

With the significant number of young people and their purchasing power, you might have your carved niche and target market.

Successful business involves thinking ahead of the competition and foresee where the next trend is headed. Attention to the needs of this massive population of young people will keep business afloat and buoyant amid economic distress.

Entrepreneurs should know when to invest more as well as when to add new products. They should be vigilant to know when to cut down production, retrain existing workers, or employ more experienced staff strength. They should also know when to expand and consolidate the business. It is of equal importance to know when your business enthusiasm and interest have gone cold. Of equal importance is the wisdom to know when it becomes necessary to close and take a break or sell off entirely as sunset often comes to us all.

Negative changes are not entirely bad!
Changes in the political terrain, instability even the type of pandemic the world is grappling with may cause severe business confusion.
Problems and challenges could also present unexpected opportunities. The strength of the entrepreneur lies in seeing opportunities where others see difficulties.

With the onset of terrorism and a sudden upsurge in terrorist acts, religious conflict, and militancy, another door of a business opportunity may suddenly open, especially for those in the field of security. Here, business opportunities in conflict resolution, production of safety gadgets, safety provision, security training, workshops, and seminars arose and in huge demand. Such businesses opened its door and became lucrative.

The coronavirus pandemic, with its challenges, has opened various doors for new business opportunities. A new line of business has been added to meet the needs of the time. Face masks, nose masks, new drugs, vaccines, ventilators, medical sterilizers, medical waste shredders, and other equipment have opened new markets and new businesses to the organization that was not producing them before.
Equally important is aspiring business persons to nurture the instinct to identify the wolves in business environments. With people staying at home due to the virus and e-commerce taking the forefront, Ponzi schemes are gaining ground. Some of these schemes are very sophisticated that most investors may not know that they are patronizing Ponzi schemes. This pack of wolves in business has wreaked havoc to the unsuspecting new business owners or investors.

Business owners need to be ahead of their games. They should think and act like the proverbial lizard that says he intuitively knows the person's movement that plans to hurl stone on it.

Like the lizard, the entrepreneur should develop the sixth sense to sniff out the wolves in business.

Trust in business should be a product of experience, loyalty, and forthrightness gained in previous relationships. It must be built over time from individuals or organizations that have proven to be reliable. Yet caution must be exercised as risk from the trust must be calculated before giving it.

Trust cheaply given has been the bane that has resulted in the collapse of many profitable businesses. As the old saying goes, you don't know a good guy by his hat's color. Trust should be a product of past dealings and previous business relationships.

The businessman who wants to run his business on an uncharted course of trust based on friendship, religion, other sentiments, and emotional attachments can be ready to fold up his business.

Experience has shown that people change over time. That your old school mate or former colleague was very reliable five years ago is not a criterion for your unalloyed trust in him handing him a compassionate position, assignment, or contract.

In-between those years, a lot may have happened. You may not know what has transpired in him during the years you were not in touch. Put a mechanism in place that will safeguard your company should trust be betrayed. Tread cautiously as you build and rebuild trust.

Beware of wolves in business.

There are business wolves. Wolves are known to be very cunning animals; unfortunately, many wolves launder themselves in the business environment waiting for novice and soft target to prey upon. These business wolves study you, your strengths and weaknesses, interests, needs, and then game on you through this information.

What makes Wolves such cunning hunters?

Wolves are nocturnal. They prefer to hunt after dusk under cover of darkness. Wolves test herds for signs of weakness, taking advantage of the very sick and old. They sniff the air for wounds or the smell of infection. Once the prey is picked, the wolves travel in the opposite direction from which the wind blows to prevent their game from catching their scent.

Wolves also observe ravens find prey—Ravens circle in the airsick animals. Circling birds means that food is close by. The wolf pack quietly will close in on their target, often in a single line. They seize their prey by the rump or the sides, preferring to attack from behind.[21]

Welcome to the business world where some of your competitors, like wolves, will take advantage of your little slip, gentle deportment, carelessness, or weakness to run you out of business.

You can learn a thing or two from the proverbial lizard – develop a sixth sense. From the wolves themselves -watch your back and never expose your weaknesses. Never become so meek to become a soft target. Please pay attention to competition even when they are moving in the opposite direction of your business.

Meeting and negotiating with suppliers.

If you are into a retailing, commodity, merchandising, manufacturing, sales, marketing, or other businesses. It is necessary, as a startup, that you acquire skills in negotiation or bargaining. This can be made more accessible if you are right in getting along with people.

A good bargain with your suppliers will add to the profit of your business. Take advantage of the volume of purchase to get a good deal. The larger the number of goods you are purchasing, the lower the per-unit fixed cost. This is where the ancient knowledge of the economy of scale comes to bear.

---

[21] Adult Sabbath school study guide. Teacher's edition. Page 71. July August, September 2009

As you focus on the immediate best deal accruable to you, consider future or long-term relationships with your suppliers on how the agreement affects them.

Always strive for a win-win situation for both parties. You may need each other in the future, and how you treat them today will determine how they may respond tomorrow.

Structure your organization where the suppliers deal with your company and not totally with an individual or representatives. This reduces the chances of individuals fraudulently cutting corners. It also comes on handy when an individual responsible for dealing with suppliers leaves your organization suddenly. Your organization will continue to move effectively and efficiently because it is not reliant on an individual or group of individuals.

However, if the company is so small that it needs to be an individual delegated to deal with that responsibility with suppliers, as a startup, get involved directly or indirectly with your leading suppliers.

It would be best if you did not delegate this area totally to an individual. Because if you do, the supplier may build a relationship with the person you commissioned instead of with the company. What then happens if the person suddenly leaves your organization? You may end up trying to reestablish a new relationship. It is more beneficial for your suppliers to deal directly with your company.

Sometimes when you are short on fund or emergency demands, you may call suppliers to send some goods to your firm even without making an immediate payment. This is possible because a relationship has been established with your company; this will be difficult if you had delegated totally to an employee who suddenly quits.

Chapter 15
BREAKING THE BACKBONE OF FAILURE

Entrepreneur and Business

For your new business to succeed, a lot will depend on you. Are you daring enough to try new things, new ways? Can you make personal sacrifices over and over and defer short term gratification for the long term benefit?

How much time, patient, drive, and creative attention, are you willing to invest in the new idea? What skill do you possess, and what unique skill can you work harder to acquire within a given time? Will you be committed enough to make an extra effort to learn in the business

Do not be half baked in your choosing field but dare to be the best in what you do because that's where the breaks are made. Opportunity seeks out for the best. Opportunities abound today as such; stay viable to benefit from new trends. Always dare to go the extra mile, which is where the promotions are received.

The Igbos of eastern Nigeria are known to be very enterprising and equally known to excel in any enterprise they channel their energies into. It is the same revelation wherever they find themselves across the globe, which brings us to the big question. What drives them?

The Igbos rarely see business or entrepreneurship as risk-taking, as emphasized in business schools, entrepreneurship hubs, and skill acquisition centers. They embrace it as one embraces and cares for a lover –with tenderness, attention, and care, not risk! Isn't love risky? But how often is love equated to risk-taking? Who thinks of risks when embarking on a love affair despite the usually attendant heartbreaks?

To the Igbos, business means seed planting, meeting needs, competition, empowerment, responsibility, goal, vision, dream, and attainment, striving to consolidate and overtake but rarely a risky venture. When you prepare your land properly, your seeds will germinate. When it sprouts, you nurture them to the extent you can guarantee a good harvest. Occasional natural disasters and other circumstantial occurrences apart, no farmer considers planting a risk.

Hence no one competes with a mindset of risk. You go to give someone a run for his money. Therefore you prepare very well, which is why Igbos spends years training and preparing correctly in their chosen interests of entrepreneurship. Not because it is a risk.

BUSINESSES DON'T ALWAYS FAIL, BUT ENTREPRENEURS FAIL MOST TIME

Four-fifths of all new businesses will fail within two years of opening. Another statistics says 65 percent of SMEs fail within three years of startup.

The statistics above are scary and discouraging, but you allow battle because of fear of death. Fear means that you prepare better, if possible, above your strength before considering and embarking on it.

It may be necessary to stop here and consider some reasons for failed businesses.

Why do businesses fail?

Business failure stems from the human factor in which poor business knowledge is the main factor.

A bright idea needs brilliant knowledge and a robust experience to blossom. Most new businesses are started with limited knowledge of the business. This is tested and tried a recipe for failure. It is also part of this book's reason to help you avoid those pitfalls that will destabilize the efforts of Streetpreneurs (Street Entrepreneurs).

In business, competent management is essential. The business is poorly managed; despite the volume of funds invested, high quality of the product, great marketing, and sales potential, the business may fail eventually. It would help if you had the right mix of a team with the right experience, competence, and blend to navigate the stormy waters of starting and delivering success.

This does not, in any way, undermine the importance of funds to the business. Anyone who plays down the significance of funds in a new business does so to his detriment and peril.

Funding is a significant challenge faced by new businesses. There is a need to work out how to raise more funds when needed.

Good knowledge of finance will be an advantage. It does great good to have a working knowledge of financial instruments.

Accountability and total separation of personal needs from that of the business are essential at inception. This involves cutting off spending that may be unhealthy and unnecessary to the new business. As noted earlier, delayed gratification is essential for the survival of the new business.

One of the important factors that often gets neglected in business is the failure to take patent, trademark, and copyright for inventions or products. This failure comes at a high cost.

Such failure causes others to exploit the child of your brain, invention, or products, which causes loss of huge revenues that would have come as benefits.

Delay to get a patent for your product or invention may mean that another 'fast guy' may take copyright or patent before you. The implication is that you may end up losing the ownership of your invention to another individual or organization.

Years ago, I was told of a guy that produced television antennae that made reception of both television and radio channels clearer and more audible. The antenna was in very high demand in the market; unfortunately, the owner never patented his invention. The technology for the antenna was simple, so others started producing the same product. He saw his product being sold in different places, yet he was not the one that made them, and eventually, he was out of business.

Not long ago, I went with Shaka, a family friend to Chinegado, who runs an automobile tires business. As the tires were being fixed, Shaka brought up a conversation about a dent on his car that caused concern. Shaka had taken the car to various experts who recommended the outright repainting of the car. Each said removing the dented spot alone will damage the car's original painting in that particular spot; as such, they advised repainting the affected areas damaged by the dent.

Shaka didn't want the car repainted; he sought a solution to remove the stain in the affected spot without defacing the original color. Chinegado said he knew a man who has a product that could do precisely that. My friend, who had heard from experts, reluctantly agreed. Calls were made, and in minutes, Baffour arrived with his product. On arrival, he took a quick look at the dent. He declared with a guarantee that his product will remove the stain without ruining the original color. Shaka, on hearing the assurance and of guarantee, thought Baffours' confidence in his product was worth trying. About thirty minutes later, after Baffour had applied his product, the dent was gone, and the original color restored!

Baffour said the idea came about three years ago by a bout of inspiration when he was facing dare financial problems and sought to develop something that might alleviate his financial situation. As they say, the rest is history, and the products have proven so effective and successful.

So far, Baffour is still the only person marketing that good product. The packaging needs improvement, and of course, the product has no patent registration. It is in danger of being stolen by another smart business wolf someday if he delays. Whoever first took patent of an invention becomes the legal owner of that product.

Products and inventions are protected by patent and copyright laws. When this is done, anyone that tries to copy or duplicate that invention without your knowledge or permission will be liable to the strong arm of the law.

Here is a brief but precise explanation of these laws, so you do not infringe on them. Those who neglect these laws lose ownership of their product as a result of ignorance.

■ Copyright Laws

These laws are made to protect materials like intellectual properties, audio and visual products, and images from those who use other people's materials as if it is their own. This also means that you will be held liable if you copy another person's materials without permission and acknowledgment and claim ownership of such. This is called plagiarism.

■ Trademark

These are laws that prevent others from using the original manufacturer's logo, Business Name, inventions, etc. This also means that you will be held liable if you use that of others. Sometimes people use others' logo or business name deceptively.

There are various ways crooks interfere deceptively with trademarks that are not theirs. They often perpetrate such, especially on brands that have been tested and have carved niche in their industry, to con customers into believing that their fake is from this reliable organization.

Often they affix another company's name or logo to their product to deceive the markets into thinking they are representing the original owner of the product while they are not.

They alter the logo or name in a way that may not be easily noticed without close observation. This is trademark Infringements that pushes such impostors into legal trouble.

■ Patent

Patent laws give every accredited company the sole official rights to use, make, and sell their product or invention. Any other person that tries to produce a patented product or invention without proper permission will be held liable.

The buildup of the above present strong reasons why businesses fail. Often, businesses don't just fail; instead, it is the entrepreneur who fails and crashes the business in most cases. A paradigm shift from business failure to entrepreneurs' loss is a significant determinant in business success or failure.

A thriving business may die or fail within three years, majorly because of the entrepreneur's decisions and not necessarily because the business is not viable. In such a situation, it is the entrepreneur that failed, not the business.

Communicating this message effectively may energize entrepreneurs to understand that their businesses' success rests mostly and squarely on them. This is not to say that businesses don't fail due to other factors other than the entrepreneur.

Let's take this example: suppose you build a four-bedroom duplex with the best quality materials, renowned building engineers, quantity surveyors, architects, and other experts that contributed to a perfect finish.

But during the development of the structure, you decided to leave a giant oak tree in front of the building to provide shade and beauty.

Later as time went on, you decided and craved more sunlight, wind, open view, and also came the need for grasses in the place as field and even a swimming pool nearby. So you decide the Oaktree should go down. Still, instead of getting a professional hand to bring down the tree, you choose to engage the cheap service of unskilled men neglecting the fact that more expertise is needed to bring down a tree close to a building.

Based on your decision for unskilled cheap labor to cut down the tree, it landed on your duplex, causing huge damage that requires lots of money to renovate the building.

Considering the huge financial involvement it will take to renovate or rebuild, which you are unprepared for, you choose to either luck down the premises or put up the property for sale. The question is, did this building collapse on its own, or is it the owner of the building that crashed a solidly constructed building due to poor decision?

65 PERCENT OF SMES WILL FAIL WITHIN THREE YEARS OF STARTUP

Demystifying the 65% statistics:

The stats say 65 percent of SMEs will fail within three years of startup).

This 65% statistic is not hard-pressed on the percentage caused by the entrepreneur's error, that is, errors caused by entrepreneurs themselves!

Suppose available records have it that 65% of startups will fail within three years. In that case, the implication is that only 35% of startups will succeed in three years! Over the years, my observations in failed small businesses and startups often show the entrepreneur the silent culprit. These issues could be due to attitude, poor decision, lifestyles, knowledge, conduct, or comportment. A situation often endangers other factors and leads to business collapse.

Let's say the 35% rate of success is constant, and of the 65% that will fail, I will propose that about 50% (of that 65%) may be due to human error, that is, entrepreneurs' failure.

That is, half of 65% (or 32.5%) will be due to human error. It also means that had the emphasis been on the strength and power of the entrepreneur to achieve business success! That means that the other half of the 65% (32.5%) will be attributed to business failure due to environmental issues, policies, economic challenges, and other factors.

Had the entrepreneur got his 32.5% right, it would have freed that additional 32.5% to the original 35% that succeeded, totaling a 67.5% rate of business success. In comparison, business failure resulting from factors other than the entrepreneurial failings would have stood at 32.5%.

With these statistics, many may embrace a startup without the acute fear of failure associated with entrepreneurship. They are now more aware that the chances of success rest almost solely on the individual running the startup. This realization will lure more people to business and likewise make business success inevitable.

Honesty is capital; invest in it.

Many businesses also fail because the business owner fails to live up to trust bestowed or expected of them. As noted earlier, trust is built over time as a result of previous relationships.

Your word ought to be your bond. Your word should be your verbal capital (things you gain because people trust your words)

When you make a promise, it has to be honored. If you are given a loan facility, or someone lends you money, the honest thing to do is repay it and at an agreed time. Suppose, due to unforeseen circumstances, things do not go as you intended, communicate with your lender as soon as possible. In that case, he may be disappointed, but there are chances of him listening and may make concessions. If eventually, he does, do not fail on your obligation again.

Do not take people's kindness for granted because once you leave that kind of impression, it may be challenging to gain their trust again, a massive loss to your relationship, business, or career.

When you do business with people, please do not be greedy; give your partner what is due. Keep your side of the bargain; over time, people may trust you, and you build trust with them.

Always secure yourself by a legal agreement that could be binding to both parties. Of course, the legal ties may not guarantee a hundred percent safety net. Still, it provides a stable platform that keeps knocking all those involved into line, providing a base to make legal demand as the need arises.

Remember, there are many wolves in business, and things are not always what they seem. So do not convict a man gentlemanly because he is in a suit or looks like a gentleman.

Learn to train and listen to your senses to sniff out the wolves. Our minds intuitively give out alarm and warning signals, which are frequently ignored because we have not observed, trained, and trusted these senses.

There is no atheist in the fox hole.
As an entrepreneur, there will be a time you need additional aid from a source other than you; miracles still do happen.

Of course, we live in a time that science not only rules but science is trusted more. As such, whatever that cannot be verified through scientific procedures, empirical evidence, or to some extent, logic will be brutally rejected even when the evidence is compelling. Sometimes things happen that defy natural laws. It may come as an unusual opportunity or an extraordinary chain of events.

With buzz words in a town like growth hacking, leverage, synergy, proactive, client control, cultural entrepreneur, social capital, new normal, disruptive innovation, monetization strategy, quick win, pivot and press on, content is king, result-oriented, vertical strategy, move the needle, innovation, Big data, deep dives, virtualization, free-hanging fruits etcetera. It looks old fashion to state believe in a God as part of success tips.

A business may improve if these buzz words are effectively applied, but there is a God thing, and the new business owner may need to tap into it. It does not make you old fashion but delivers flourishing business.

There is a divine intervention out there, an intervention that does not follow natural laws.

Excelling in your chosen Endeavour may not be solely in your hands. Those things called happy accidents might not be accidents after all, which is where God's things or miracles come in.

The God factor does not preclude you from doing your part; you have to make yourself available by being committed, passionate, and good at your chosen interest or profession.

Hard work and excellent skills must meet a great opportunity to flourish. Remove that great opportunity, and your effort will be mere labor. God performs a miracle and opens a great opportunity for you with that which is in your hand.

Sometimes you may do everything right but lack that killer opportunity that seems to drop out from nowhere, which is an unusual opportunity through which real change comes.

A God thing will be needed to achieve success even when the odds are against you.

Despite skills, capacity, training, preparedness, professionalism, the volume of the fund, knowledge of individual and teams, and collective skills, there really will be that time you need a power other than you to execute a task and succeed.

In most cases, you may not be able to explain how things suddenly worked in your favor. How you came across that one person whom you did not go in search of but whom your break-through or your turn-around stems from.

This is an act of God or divine intervention. Although some may call such a happy accident, chance encounters, fortune, or luck, it does not matter what it is called; miracles still happen!

Footballers, for example, usually prefer speaking of additional luck! A very good team may hit the bar in three one on one situations with the goalkeeper. There are instances where the best strikers ballooned the ball away while faced with an empty net. We have seen good players getting their n goals against their teams in defending, own goals that decide the game. Others have kicked the ball towards the atmosphere even during penalty shootouts. You begin to wonder about the connection between the atmosphere and a post.

Some occasions see inferior opponents scoring at the only chance they have, perhaps at the ninetieth minute, and end up carrying the day winning the trophy!

Even nature occasionally does intervene, playing a part in winning. We have witnessed the wind carrying the ball dazzling the goalkeeper. In contrast, the ball swerves and curves as it is lodged inside the opponent's net. Refereeing decision helps to secure winnings not because the referee is partial but because he was not correctly positioned to see clearly.

Again how did you survive where your friends who swim better than you drowned even when you cannot swim, yet somehow you survived the tide. How did you survive that ghastly accident or that bomb explosion while everyone around you died?

At other times, how come you are HIV negative while your partner is positive, even when you both have been on it unprotected? It can't just be a chance occurrence.

There will come a time in business and other life situations when you may need that additional support other than you.

Chapter 16

GETTING FULFILED AND GENERATING JOBS

Study quietly as you do your own business
And work with your own hands…
That you may walk honestly
Toward them that are without
That you may have lack of nothing.
–Paul

"Running start up is like eating glass, you start to like the taste of your own blood" The above quotes are credited to Sean Parker, the Man who earlier helped launched Facebook and later created Airtime, an investment of $33million that failed in 2012.

Of course, we understand that running a startup is a personal interest worth its commitments. However, it is a stormy sea where resolve and focus are essential recipes for success.

Our era has never needed Streetpreneurs as we need them at this period of our history.

With resources being depleted at an alarming rate and the government increasingly helpless and unable to provide the much-needed job to move the masses away from the poverty line.

Through small-scale enterprise, entrepreneurship becomes pivotal in providing the platform to move the people from poverty to wealth creation, thereby entrenching a sustainable, productive, and prosperous independent lifestyle.

Entrepreneurship gives the masses the needed lifeline that accelerates the emergence of a burgeoning middle-class society.

Nigeria is a country of budding talents in arts, craft, trade, merchandise, and to no small extent, invention. A society loaded with men and women of creative ingenuity from a poor background, minimal education, and lack of general government support, continues to generate jobs.

Jobs created by these youths are often far below their potential and capacity due to a lack of government support, especially in necessary infrastructures.

Emphasis on entrepreneurship supported by deliberate government policy programs and interventions to lift the masses out of poverty can turn around any economy for good.

Interestingly, across Africa and globally, there are existing platforms to build a prosperous world economy; a focused and committed leadership that can meet this expectation in record time is needed in this time of world history.

There is an urgent need for citizens' education to think of Street entrepreneurship as the best option to activate and restart the economy after the global lockdown. An approach tends to bring about citizens enlightenment on a new attitude in the way things are to be done in this era, other than how things were done in the past. The past led to over-reliance on government for job creation, a dependency on paid employment that failed the citizenry. Any plan to rebuild small businesses must target the people through robust support tailored strategically to SME's.

The Lucky Bamboo as a Metaphor for Entrepreneurship

I had visited my friend Sawa that day, and I was admiring his beautifully spiraled lucky bamboo. He took his time and explained what it took to get the spirals we all enjoy having in our homes.

Entrepreneurs are generally known to be planners, tactical, innovative people, and risk-takers. They are often adaptable to changes and with a passion that always motivates them to keep going. They are knowledgeable in their business interest or products.

To the entrepreneur, money management is a skill, a lifestyle, and a need. Most entrepreneurs are avid planners who also know how to take chances and to spot opportunities.

I will immediately use the example of a Chinese plant as sent to me by Sawa in explaining what it takes to be entrepreneurial-minded.

The Lucky Bamboo (Fu Gwey Zhu)

The Chinese often identify themselves with the bamboo as a symbol of strength and fortitude. The resilient bamboo proves that it can withstand the turmoil of a storm and survives unscathed. To get this beautiful plant with the spirals and waves, the hardworking and patient Chinese must exhibit the following traits.

- Diligence

- Efficient

- Innovation

- Commitment

- Perseverance

A quick search of my HP Laptop dictionary gives meaning to these words

DILIGENCE	EFFICIENT	INNOVATIVE	COMMITMENT	PERSEVERANCE
Assiduousness	Well organize	Pioneering	Promise	Insistence
Industry	Competent	Inventive	Pledge	Urgency
Meticulous	Resourcefulness	Original	Vow	Firmness
Thoroughness	Proficient	New	Obligation	Resolve
Attentive	Capable	Modern	Binder	Determination
Carefulness	Good at your job	Ground breaking	Dedication	
	Professional	Novel	Loyalty	

The above traits are the reasons the Chinese are thriving today.

How are lucky bamboo plants grown to achieve those exotic waves and spiral shapes? Sawa continued:

The plants are first grown in a plastic pot.

A furrow is plowed into the clay-like soil at a 45-degree angle and the shade house's length.

The Lucky bamboo plants in the plastic grown pot are then laid at its side in this furrow at a 45-degree angle.

Periodically, about every month, the Lucky bamboo plants are rotated 15 degrees. This same process is repeated until the desired shape is reached.

This sometimes takes up to two years. The Chinese have a lot of hardworking people and are extremely patient.

It is of little surprise why the Chinese economy is today with the unimaginable turn around they have witnessed in a little over two decades. Any nation or people with those traits need only the right policy and its leadership's commitment to be in pole position in nations' comity.

Many Asian Countries have proven what a blend of industry, bold action, and detailed economic development plan can achieve when selfishness is traded for selflessness. They have shown that when self-interest makes way to focused leadership, a leadership aimed at service to the nation and the people, great strides will be attained in good time.

Business is too important to be left solely in the hands of entrepreneurs. No country will do well or achieve significant progress if the business is left in entrepreneurs' hands, no matter how smart the entrepreneurs. This suggests that successful entrepreneurship needs good policy and initiative to thrive.

There are various ways that the government can provide support to help young people engaged in small businesses.

Young entrepreneurs should be trained in different areas, which include:

- Customer relations

- Marketing of their products

- Emphasis on the importance of having neat finishing for their product to meet international standards and, as such, compete with other products globally. This is an area usually taken for granted, especially among uneducated small business owners.

- Receive training from export promotion councils, as many think exporting goods and services are very complex issues made for the big organizations.

- Trained to apply for government contracts in a merit-based contract award system. Bold policies and new legislation should be enacted to effect positive change in procedures and award of contracts. This should be taken entirely away to neutral organizations from where the contract originates.

Intellectual property and inventions should have strong legislative protection and backing to encourage individuals to test their ideas, knowing that they will reap a reward if they eventually succeed. The next chapter will further explore this topic.

Chapter 17

NEED FOR ENTREPRENEURSHIP COLLABOR

By entrepreneurship "collabor," I mean collaboration between government and entrepreneurs. Just as many entrepreneurs can do without good government policies, interventions, and especially the ease of doing business.

Global entrepreneurship monitor (GEM) is a London-based research project on an annual assessment of the national level of entrepreneurial activity in diverse countries. GEM conducts the world's largest study of entrepreneurship dynamics, conducting a yearly survey in 99 countries. The result shows that Africa abounds with business-minded people.

The survey also uncovers that Nigerians, in particular, possess more business enthusiasm than the rest of the world.

According to the report:

90% of Nigerian adults strongly believe they have the skill to run their own business.

35% of Nigerians are already involved in one entrepreneurial activity or the other

44% of Nigerians plans to launch their own business within the next five years

The surveys also revealed that 82% of Nigerians youths see the entrepreneur as a good career.

Going by that report, Nigeria is an entrepreneurial nation that needs good and deliberate government policies to harness and feed this potential. The impact of strategically structured small and medium businesses will move the country to unprecedented job creation height.

Government has the responsibility to provide an enabling environment, infrastructure, security, stable policies that support, motivate, attract, and protect investors and their investments.

Tax waivers may be needed to attract investors; it is government alone that can provide such support.

Politics is also too important to be left solely in the hands of politicians.

A nation with little or no natural resources but a focused leadership with vision will achieve better in the long run than a country with abundant rich natural resources with no strategy for real sector development.

The story of Dubai's transformation from a mere arid land to a beautiful modern city that attracts the high and mighty across the globe is general knowledge. In our lifetime Singapore transformed from a Third World economy with no natural resources to one of the wealthiest cities.

Africa needs the right mix of political leaders to include majorly young people to move the desired destination content. Entrepreneurship has to be encouraged to flourish.

Most Nigerians are generally hardworking people full of hope and optimism, a people that frown on idleness. You see them doing different kinds of small businesses without government support to sustain themselves and their families.

From Aba to Umuahia, Owerri to Onitsha, Port-Harcourt to Enugu, Calabar, Akwa-Ibom, Lagos, Ibadan, Jos, Kaduna, Kano to Yola are floats of small businesses that provide the needed jobs for these teaming population.

A bold strategic action plan needs to be put in place by the government to steer small businesses to create a buoyant economy. Coming up with innovations that will fast track the establishment of viable and flourishing small businesses will be a sure way to achieve the vision of a prosperous nation.

A prosperous economy will not be delivered by the government alone. Still, a viable economy is built by small businesses in an environment that will attract foreign direct investment (FDI).

According to the 2019 United Nations estimates, the current Nigerian population is over 198,902,448 people, about 2.6% of the total world population, and a median age of 17.9.

Wikipedia puts Nigeria's youth age at 18-30 years with a youth population of over 33,652,424 members.

By implication, the Nigerian population has exceeded two hundred million as of the end of 2019!

Other agencies have estimates of the broader youth population and an unemployment crisis. Over fifty-five percent of these youths are either unemployed or underemployed.

Again it is worthy of emphasis to note that government alone through the public sector cannot, despite the effort, create enough jobs for its entire citizenry. It is the private sector that drives the fulfillment of a robust working-class society. A strategy that favors and attracts small business and foreign investors remains an ideal solution to job creation.

The entertainment industry, music, and Nollywood provide the wonder of what the private sector can achieve, with Nigeria Nollywood being ranked 3rd in the world after Hollywood and Bollywood. The industry in itself could generate massive job opportunities for citizens as it permanently empowers many youths to be self-reliant. This could be achieved by organizing the industry to create much-improved quality content. The entertainment industry has the knack to identify talents and skills lying waste in the streets. When the industry is supported by the government, it will provide a robust and lofty avenue to launder the country's good image and provide a better narrative of the Nigerian people.

The entertainment industry has different departments and crew that come together in making movies. These mean that there are specialized skills required for youths to take the training. Such areas include directing, production management, casting, camera operation and lighting, special effects, sound engineers and technicians, production accounting, film editing, and visual effect editors, animation crews, costume, makeup and hair designers, location crew, script department, digital imaging experts, motion control operators, art directors, and production designers, graphic and design artists, prop makers and of course the actors and the actresses we see on our screens. This is to mention but a few jobs, training, and skills generated from the Nollywod industry.

These skills can also be used elsewhere other than the movie industry to raise a self-dependent and entrepreneurial society. Attention to the sector will bring about a conglomerate, skilled empowerment of citizens.

The well-structured entertainment industry will drive in the much needed foreign exchange and deconstruct the flawed narrative that has left Nigeria's wrong impression and Nigerians.

Most Nigerians crave the desire to be liberated financially and live the good life. They have identified education and entrepreneurship as a means to achieve this independence. They travel and migrate to different countries under harsh conditions in the hope of a better life. They often achieve these lofty self-set goals and help build their host countries' economies through their entrepreneurial spirit.

This desire to be financially liberated that shuns dependency on government is part of Nigerians' high entrepreneurial spirit. What is needed is a little nudge by government that will trigger self-reliance.

The government can start by providing infrastructure, affordable education, financial and non-financial incentives, and grants to support this hunger to be job creation and self-employed citizens.

Each year, a country that gets over two million job seekers added to the already flooded job market needs to be intentional on its policies. With a youth population where about fifty-two percent is either unemployed or underemployed, Nigeria has a leeway to use what is on the ground to empower most of this great population.

It is safe to see entrepreneurship as an inherent potential for a large number of the population. To a large extent, Nigerians are not people to be persuaded to be entrepreneurs; entrepreneurship is part of their natural gift and talent. What is needed is a government that provides necessary facilities that bring about a functional society of SMEs.[22] Once these basics services are provided, Nigerians need a little nudge to excel. This can be achieved by taking advantage of what works for the people to get the best out.

Nigerians are very religious by nature. The clerics whose words are often taken to heart by their members and adherent should be incorporated and made to receive training in best approaches; such training aims to encourage their adherents to use facilities judiciously and responsibly as they embrace entrepreneurship.

Worship places, faith-based and non-faith-based organizations, and civil society groups have to be encouraged to come up with talent hunt programs. An all-inclusive hunt is other than those carried out by show biz outfits that concentrate and gears towards music, dance, reality entertainment programs, and events.

The faith-based and non-faith-based organization will encourage its members to embrace mechanized agriculture, ICT,

---

[22] *Small medium enterprise*

manufacturing of light equipment, vocational training, and other apprenticeships such as furniture making, mechanics, farming, clothes making, baking, arts and crafts, poultry business, and shoe production. Emphasis should be made on good finishing that meets global standards, which has been lacking.

Those men and women of great creative ingenuity and uncommon talents worldwide in places like Aba in Abia state make quality handbags, shoes, clothing, inventions like electrical and electronic components, and different technological products.

Others at Nnewi in Anambra State have mastered the art of making motor spare parts, manufacture scientific equipment, automobiles, chemical processing, and plastic manufacturers.

Sculptors and other crafts in Benin, textiles in Kaduna, Ibadan, and leather tanning in Kano, should all be encouraged to produce a good and topmost finish that meets the global standard that products good enough to be cherished at home and abroad.

The export promotion council, State, and the federal chamber of commerce, trade and industry, Technology and business incubation centers, and other relevant agencies can then provide assistance, guidance, and training to get these products to a good standard and introduced to specific international markets.

Nigeria, with her over 300 ethnic groups, each ethnic group is unique and peculiar in their mode of dressing, culture, ceremonies, festivals, foods, and business. This ethnic strength and specialty is also an avenue for job creation.

Some ethnic groups are known to be better in merchandise. In contrast, others are endowed with natural resources like solid and liquid minerals, rubber, cotton fishing, and agriculture.

Others are better known for palatable dishes, soul-inspiring songs, and music, beautiful and engaging festivals, use of local and foreign musical instruments, carpentry, textile, tie and die, local gin, local juice zobo, kunu, palm wine, palm oil, and others with local skills and talents.

Effective and efficient traditional medicine, robust, rich culture, leather tanning, nomadic life of cattle rearing, knitting, arts, and craft. There are also local security personnel, better chauffeurs' and even very reliable house helps have been noted as strength of some specific localities and cultures. It is even said that some ethnic groups are known to be more romantic than others.

Through entrepreneurship, further developments and job creation can be created through this primordial ethnic strength, with an upgrade where their traditional technologies and values can be improved upon.

The universities and other tertiary institutions have to wake up to the responsibilities of providing knowledge-based, high technologies like biotechnology processing, information, and communication technology (ICT), Robotics, Space technology, artificial intelligence (AI), Laser technology, Nanotechnology, and other advanced technologies that will drive a more holistic scientific economy for the future.

Policies that encourage research should be introduced, and lecturers motivated and engaged in exchange programs with other global intuitions of specific identified interests.

Successful Businessmen, especially those with humble beginnings, should be encouraged to volunteer their services or experiences to inspire students, undergraduates, and other organized interest groups.

Sponsorship programs should be established to help those with good business plans, blueprints, fertile ideas, and dreams to achieve such lofty programs.

With the advantage of telecom outfit and internet facilities at our fingertips, one can now browse with little or no cost.

People who can read should be encouraged to upgrade their ideas and learn from the internet instead of using the web negatively. They can take advantage of all these resources and develop a budding business that can be exported abroad.

Empowering the youths improves the quality of life and living standards of all. To get Nigeria to the next level, where institutions work to full strength and capacity, is the first sign of a country that hopes to get it right.

Nigeria can take a cue from different established economies with a similar history that was once contemporaries but has gotten it right to develop its economy. They can also glean from established and prosperous economies. This will help draw a program based on peculiar challenges, environmental needs, and unique ethnic strength.

In some of these economies, small businesses spearheaded quantum growth that culminated in a flourishing and booming economy.

For example, in the United States, it is evident that small business provides the backbone for its thriving economy. Here, the small business provides the bulk of employment of that country. Consider the following examples:

■ About 99% of all American business is small.

- Small business provides approximately 75% of the net new jobs added to the US economy every year.

- Small business represents 99.7% of all employees

- Small business employs 50.1% of all private workforces

- Small business provides 40.9% of private sales in the country[23]

Looking at the above statistics, it will be economic suicide to ignore small businesses in any Country. A responsive government must provide a framework for a prosperous small business environment.

On their part, the Asia continent has provided the world with a modern-day surprise of how an economy can be turned around within a few decades. Such government decides to match words with action.

Nigeria is one of the members of MINT (Mexico, Indonesia, Nigeria, and Turkey) Nations. On her part, talking tough must be backed by visible action plans that are workable. Plans that will sustain industrialization and rapid innovation just as the BRICKS (Brazil, Russia, India, China and later South Africa) nations have demonstrated, that determined and progressive strategies and indeed, a focused nation can squeeze out a sizeable global economic power from the developed economies to meet her aspirations.

More so, bold and deliberate reforms are still needed in the banking sector; this sector provides the pillar for economic growth. I look forward to a time of one digit interest rate that will power business growth. Wherever the banking sector is shaky and unstable, it reflects the economic imbalance of such a country. A strong banking sector is capable of moving any economy at a pace

---

[23] Hector V. Barreto. US Small Business Administrator.

intended. Fortunately, Nigeria has an innovative and Technology-driven banking industry.

Africa needs a radical revolution in the educational sector for the vision of a great country. By extension, a great continent is expected to be a reality. This must involve the right blend of vocational education to academic work where skills are also emphasized.

The need to inculcate vocational education into the tertiary curriculum becomes a solely rigid option that should be embraced. Of course, we know this has already been considered and often introduced. Still, the remaining challenge is making it truly functional.

To be part of the information era, there is a need to find that pathway to merging two education; academic education and professional education. This, I firmly believe this will propel economic growth and lead to a jump towards a technology that truly targets the fourth industrial revolution.

Nigeria must emphasize merit because this can bring a buoyant economy where creativity is allowed, engineered to thrive, and blossom, irrespective of where the idea originates.

Entrepreneurship must be introduced in the curriculum and allowed to work, perform, and achieve objectives. This is essential where undergraduates are exposed to self-reliance right from their time in schools.

Brainstorming and thinking out of the box helps students to horn ideas that could create opportunities when applied.

Students have to be trained and tutored to education, inspiring them to develop their ideas and solutions to problem-solving. This should be the focal point of entrepreneurial education.

A funding system covering sponsorship, training, nurture, and business incubation will lift ideas off the sketch to workshops. Such an established system gives wings for viable ideas to translate to realistic opportunities and creativity. By so doing, smart individuals will be excited to open the kimono and display their lofty creativities.

Successful entrepreneurs and other business owners should be inculcated into the school system and given roles or occasionally invite them to institutions on speaking engagements.

Businessmen and industrialist industrialists will then have an interactive session with undergraduates as this brings more inspiration and awareness. It can also open up these young people's minds to know that already existing business and a corporation can be made far better than what is on the ground.

Nigerians being industrious, energetic, hardworking, and enthusiastic people have to be encouraged to embrace ICT and related business, integrated cloud and software technologies, call centers, and off-shore outsourcing of data from Europe, the United Kingdom, the US, and even some Asia, African countries and across the globe. This will require digital transformation that emphasizes professionalism, expertise, commitment, trustworthiness, and the inclination to do the job better and cheaper to attract hefty patronage from outside this country's shores.

Youths are better off to explore these avenues for job creation even while within the walls of tertiary institutions.

Nigeria can take advantage of its vast youth population to drive an industrial economy where labor and production costs are cheaper than many others in the West and some Asia economies. This can also attract more investors who will take advantage of low production costs to establish industries that will produce wealth and job creation.

Politicians ought not to be left out in this holistic turnaround. The need for responsible and transparent management of resources provides the engine to move these development plans and strategies to the *permanent-site.[24]

Government has to work towards the entrenchment of fair policies that will create more mega entrepreneurs in the cadre of Aliko Dangote of Dangote Group, Innocent Chukwuma of Innoson Motor Vehicle, Frank Nneji Of ABC Transport, Tony Elumelu - Chairman Transnational Corporation of Nigeria Plc (Transcorp) and the likes of Mike Adenuga of Globacom, Atiku Abubakar of Intels Nigeria Ltd and ABTI Schools and Jim Ovia of Zenith Bank.

These mega entrepreneurs can create a great number of jobs while ushering international attention, recognition, and investment partnerships, which project the good image of the country.

The fascinating revelation is that most of these Forbes recognized mega entrepreneurs today were once street entrepreneurs. This is another strong reason why policy creation that will facilitate the emergence of Streetpreneurs is the way forward in the post-Covid-19 era.

Disruptive Innovation

This innovation creates a new market by providing a new set of values, which ultimately (and unsuspected) overtakes an existing market. Put another way, disruptive innovations are the innovation

---

[24] *our shared desired destination*

that creates a new market and value network that eventually disrupts an existing market, displacing established market-leading firms, products, and alliances.[25]

Bringing innovations to already existing businesses

Whereas it is good to come up with new and fresh ideas in business, it is good to bring innovation, sanity, and order to existing ones. Man is a creature of improvement and one that keeps striving for perfection. There is always a need to bring innovation to already existing businesses.

One of my favorites, Vince Lombardi Jr., quotes remain.

"Gentlemen, we will chase perfection, and we will chase it relentlessly, knowing all the will we can never attain it, along the way we shall catch excellence."

As we have them today, an automobile's luxury may have had its origin as a mere four-wheeled vehicle with a combustion engine! Later through the French army came a steam-powered road transport vehicle.

Further simultaneous innovations by Germans brought about a genuinely modern gasoline/petrol-powered internal combustion engine as we have it today with Karl Benz taking patent of his Benz Patent-Motorwagen.

---

[25] https//en.m.wikipedia.org/wiki/disruptive innovation

American Henry Ford later invented a massed produced technic of the automobile.

Today electric cars and driverless cars are further innovations witnessed in an automobile, increasing comfort, speed, and economy.

Christopher Mcfadden identifies the 20 most significant innovations and inventions of automobile engineering: from the first engine to today

1. The steam engine kicked things off

2. The internal combustion engine made cars' cheap.'

3. The starter engine rendered cranks obsolete

4. The diesel engine is pretty efficient

5. Anti-lock brakes helped to save lives

6. Automatic transmission made driving easier

7. Power steering made deriving more pleasurable

8. Airbags: saving lives with the power of the air

9. Electric car engines are a thing of the past and future.

10. GPS – US Military tech getting you from A to B

11. Catalytic converter: Improving air quality

12. Saving a life with a three-point seat belt

13. Improved fuel efficiency with the Hybrid Drivetrain

14. Stability control helped stop skids

15. Onboard diagnostic 11 (OBD11) improved engine management

16. Dual-Clutch transmission made gear shifts seamless

17. Smart key C(FOB): Effortless engine ignition

18. Turborcharges increased energy power and fuel efficiency

19. Flashing turn signals let other drivers know your intentions

20. Cruise control paved the way for driverless cars[26].

Disruptive Innovation in the Transportation Sector

Frank Nneji of ABC transport took transport business headlong in Nigeria, bringing disruptive innovation that has positively become the new normal to a business that was previously often run by touts.

Those innovational onslaughts by Frank triggered a homogenous change in the industry. They led others in that line of business to follow suit or ran out of business.

Today we see graduates working in motor transport companies with dignity. Passengers are treated like those on airplanes, and safety rules meet international standards. This was not the case before Frank and ABC Transport came on board the Nigerian transport business. That positive change captured the market for ABC transport on entering the market. Other transport companies were compelled by that wind of change to comply or lose their market to the new Transport Company. The whole country benefitted to date.

People now have confidence in road transportation, enjoying comforts as they make their trips within and outside the country. In

---

[26] *https://interestingengineering.com*

the process of enjoying beautiful views as they transverse the breath-taking scene across Nigeria, an opportunity lost when you travel by air.

In the process, ABC Transport owners created a robust tourism sector that led to other sub businesses sprout from the transport business. These sub-businesses include courier services, hotel businesses, and create job opportunities for the youths.

When ABC transport started operation and was employing graduates in a sector known to be filled with touts and illiterates, ABC transport made innovations in the sector that made it attractive. They delivered good work conditions that young graduates now see the job as respectable. Today, many other transport sectors have followed suit, and everyone is better for it.

Chapter 18

REACHING OUT AND REACHING IN FOR JOB CREATION

As job seekers' population increases, the tertiary institutions are churning out thousands of graduates each year. The system neither prepares to absorb nor think self-reliant.

On graduation, these young people enter the labor market with zeal to get employed and begin to shoulder personal responsibilities. They begin to feel the weight of the reality on the ground, a fact of unemployment.

As the years go by, unemployment's impact begins to toll on these once energetic and zealous young people.

Expectations begin to diminish, creativity gradually phases out, and confidence becomes farfetched as they begin to take whatever job presented to them instead of thinking self-reliant.

Finally, earlier dreams and aspirations dissipate, extinguished, and buried forever. The system has succeeded in destroying another of its bright brains!

Not long ago, the unemployment crisis was brought to bear when Dangote groups advertised vacant truck drivers. It was reported that among the over 13,000 applications received, includes

● 6 PHD holders

● 8646 high degree holders

● 704 Master's Degree and MBA holders, for truck drivers!

As if the above statistics are not bad enough, Nigerians wake up not too long to the infamous failed immigration aptitude test tragedy. The immigration disaster resulted in a stampede where over 750,000 Nigerians youths applied for about 4,500 job vacancies in the Nigeria Immigration Service (NIS). A job that perhaps may have all been taken by friends and cronies of senior Government officials.

In a stadium alone, it was reported that over 60,000 youths were present to write the test, which led to stamped, resulting in tens of death and hundreds of injuries. These were the case in various states in the country where stadiums were filled above capacity.

Recently, social media was trending with photos and videos of youths in their hundreds and thousands of flooding locations and streets for Big Brother Naija (BBN) audition; only 20 youths were selected. The crowd obstructed movement in nearby streets extending to Allen and Adeniyi Jones, Ikeja, leading to a stampede where many were on hospital emergency units. This is a worrying situation that should not be ignored, knowing that many others did not apply to the immigration job as much as those who used but did not go for the test.

This recent event is a wake-up call to the unemployment situation in the country.

To help curb such a situation, a developed service sector is needed to provide a much-needed job for our young people.

It is estimated that service sector firms employ about 30% of the World workforce. The good news is that the service sector can be a catalyst that pivots other economic sectors. A robust service sector will reduce the large unemployment workforce.

For example, a good financial service sector will empower investors who may depend on this sector's initial lifeline. Different large and small businesses will grow from a buoyant financial service sector. Industrialization, agriculture, technology, manufacturing, merchandise, ICT, textile, and steel, and many more organizations and firms will spring up from a stable financial sector.

The Telecommunication sector is another service sector that has provided jobs and has changed lives, and many do business. With a mobile phone, tablet, smartphone, laptop, and affordable internet access, we can do business with another person or organization on the other side of the globe in the comfort of our bedroom. Online marketing and other businesses have never been better than it is in this period.

According To U.N. Telecom Agency Report. – The World has nearly as many cell phone subscriptions as its inhabitants. The agency says there were about 6 billion subscriptions by the end of 2011 – roughly one for 86 of every 100 people. Currently, this figure would have exceeded that documented in 2011. Considering that the use of cell phones has increased today, the reason is not far-fetched.

Worldwide mobile subscription was estimated to pass the 8 billion mark as of 2019; for the first time, reaching a total of 8.3 billion mobile subscriptions worldwide, it is currently up from 7.9 billion in 2018. (Statista Feb, 2020).

Note that the U.N current world population as of august 2020 is 7.8billion

The telecom industry has opened up a vast new market that, when integrated into, generates employment. Youths should be encouraged to explore and acquire a proficient skill that will benefit them in this business line.

Other micro and sub businesses emerged through telecom, providing jobs to millions of people. The businesses include call centers, ATM services, Recharge card or air time sales out, let phone business, phone spare parts business, phone repair shops, viewing centers', soft drinks, snacks, restaurants business, and other unrelated business areas. These are, in addition to the big data related to businesses.

In many states, GSM and computer villages have emerged. These places' main business revolves around mobile phones, mobile phone sales, phone parts, and accessories. A visit to GSM locations like the Farm Centre in Kano, computer village in Lagos, GSM village in Abuja, Aba, and various other locations will reveal the impact of telecommunication on job creation. The Telecom sector has reduced drastically the cost of doing business as you may not necessarily need to travel to deliver or confirm some business. The cash movement has benefited from telecom sectors as cash transfers are now being made without visiting bank premises.

The transport service sector is another service area that can provide the needed job for the population. Such services include air transport, water, land, and train transport. Also, courier services, hotel and reservations, tourism, car hire services, motor spare part businesses, and language translation business.

Consider also textile companies, which can generate a huge amount of employment within the factory.

Such engagements will be extended to the cotton farm, markets, and various other places. Other sub businesses will come up from the textile business. A revamped textile outfit will create more employment and empower more farmers who will cultivate, harvest, and prepare cotton. The farmers will produce raw materials that will be needed in these factories.

Apart from the employment generated from spinning, processing, weaving, finishing, and marketing textile products.

The power sector is a huge employer of labor. A stable power sector will attract foreign investment and trigger the proliferation of both large and small businesses.

This sector is so needed that any economy without a reliable power sector is as good as comatose. The power sector drives real development and creates mega jobs, small businesses, and large firms. It provides energy for startups, small, medium, and large businesses. It propels the establishment of highly power-dependent large organizations, steel manufacturing companies, ceramics industries, car manufacturing companies, and other big corporations that generate big jobs.

A reliable power sector will boost business and provide gainful employment to youths. These will ameliorate the youth's restiveness. An employed youth may not be used as political thugs.

They will not be attracted to armed robbery, cybercrimes, and other societal vices. They will not be easily brainwashed by terrorists who use them for various despicable activities. The total advantages of improving these sectors will bridge the gaps between the haves and have-nots and entrench peaceful co-existence among the entire citizens.

An active small business sector can produce an enviable economy that cannot be on its knees during periods of 'down size' 'right size' when organizations fire their workforce or close down the business.

A healthy small business economy will bring about the populace's minimal impact and less chaos when agencies retrench or retire workers. A robust small business will assimilate workers that lost their jobs and provide opportunities to those willing to venture into their startup.

Empowered masses are easier to lead but difficult to manipulate, especially during the election. An explosion of small businesses can open up the emergence of a more middle-class society.

GENERATING EMPLOYMENT THROUGH AGRICULTURE

Agriculture is another huge employer of labor. A targeted effort to this sector unleashes a generation of employed masses. The government needs to place premiums in this sector to help most of its citizens out of unemployment.

Policymakers should inculcate their plans of action to establish viable government-assisted microcredit, loans, grants, and other financial incentives accessible to small, medium enterprises (SME's). Single-digit interest on loans spread over time should target those at the grassroots. This also helps to improve yield, skill, and have the wherewithal to manage their small businesses.

Tractors and other modern farm equipment, irrigation, fertilizers can be purchased by the government and lease at subsidized rates to make way for mechanized farming and make agriculture an attractive occupation for the masses.

More research in the storage of perishable products should be engaged. The government comes up with strategies to assist farmers with storages in bumper harvest time.

The government can deliver a scheme to mop up excesses yield and pay them to stop production when necessary to avoid flooding the market with agricultural products. Excess agricultural product crashes the price of the product and discourages farmers from further effort.

How can young people be encouraged to embrace farming without making it attractive to them? Without helping them with means of storage to avoid wastage when there is a great harvest.

Our business and technology incubation centers, the National Directorate of employments, Bank of Industry (BOI), National root Crops Research Institutes, National Institutes for Tropical Agriculture, Seed production and storage agencies, and other agencies of such should be made available to the masses, farmers and other entrepreneurs.

These agencies' functions and nature have to be public in clear advert messages through the radio, television, and especially via social media platforms. This should especially target programs in which the youths are involved like football matches, soap operas like the Indian, Mexican, and Philippines telenovela programs, Nollywood movies, reality television program like Big Brother Africa/ Naija, Gulder Ultimate Search, Glo Naija sings, and other programs that the youth are attracted to. Empowered masses can translate to an improved standard of living.

Chapter 19

STEPPING INTO DIGITAL ECONOMY

This chapter aims to persuade and convince the reader to use social connections to attain the desired height. Twenty-first-century global citizens should leverage the advantages and opportunities on the internet to increase their worth and productivity. The infusion of the internet and social media into business is one of the remarkable accomplishments of this digital transformed era. Facebook, with monthly active users of 2.5 billion as of the fourth quarter of 2019, has remained the biggest social network worldwide with 2.9 billion people as an active user in at least one of the company's core products like Facebook, Whatsaap, Instagram, or Messenger. You are one of those huge populations of users that could fill a continent.

The success generated from digital marketing and online business is so huge yet growing and waiting to be mined that any business ignoring the internet is not just undermining and shortchanging itself but contributing to failed businesses' statistics.

We live in a big data world as online citizens where international boundaries exist no more. The benefits of sales and visibility across network of buyers and sellers is a major advantage of this no boundary existence.

Suppose you're on any social media platform chatting, commenting, watching videos, sharing pictures, and forwarded messages. In that case, you're good enough to go. You've trained yourself without knowing it; you've gathered friends, fans, followers, and generated support groups by loving and friendly interactions. Now, it's time to leverage these platforms for business and entrepreneurial advantages.

You can sell or market, train, tutor, advertise or bring your business to the knowledge of your social group and global audience. We all need the money, and to make money, you have to sell something of value by adding value.

To be employable and functional in this digital economy era, you should be deliberate to key into the demand of the times irrespective of what you studied or your vocation. That way, you will appropriate the full benefit from being a utility player, as discussed in previous chapters. Master class courses are affordable to put you on the path of mastery of the digital economy.

The internet provides free online courses with certification that you can leverage to kick start. All you need is an android phone and data. Later you can sign up for an online Master's class for a fee.

We live in the e-world where every facet of our life, business, and recreation are now connected to the internet. Our traditional media is now digital – digital music, digital video, and digital advertising, including social media platforms and other classified adverts.

Today we have e-publishing, e-health, e-travel, e-ticketing, online shopping, e-government, smart car features, e-services, online food delivery, online dating sites, online event ticketing like sports events, and online fitness.

Smart homes are no longer luxury but necessities. We have energy management through big data, intelligent appliances, smart home entertainment, smart lighting, and security.

Today e-commerce has become the way of life where purchases and distribution, sales. Supply, buying and selling, crowd investing, digital remittance, and even Robo advisors are engaged online. This extends to financial technology or Fintech, where payments are now made digitally, POS Payment, and other digital remittance. Micro-financing is now interwoven into our everyday activities.

Cloud computing, blockchain, and virtual currency are the way in the future. Being digitally savvy could reasonably reduce the threat posed by internet hackers. You will be better equipped to detect unsecured links and risky sites.

The entrepreneur, young graduates, and even those gainfully employed will leapfrog in their careers and business when they leverage and integrate space digitally into their social interactions and businesses.

Today many businesses are harvesting huge clients from the use of technology from digital space. The statistics below will engage your mind to reconsider and embrace the digital economy.

What should be of interest is that the growth has been steady since 2011. The online market generated $35.68Bilion; as of 2015, it has grown steadily to$ a 107Billion. Online coaching marketing is projected to grow to the tune of $325billion by 2025. (Punch online 4th June 2018). Again In a 2015 survey, it was gathered that about 92% of students in tertiary institutions have an online presence.

Here in Nigerian, with a population of about 200 million, statistics show that in 2018, Nigerian online presence was 92.3 million. By May 2019, it grew to122 million. It is expected to reach 187 million by 2023.

Internet User participation in Nigeria from 2017 to 2023 is projected as follows.

2017	37.95
2018	47.1%
2019	56.4%
2020	65.15
2021	72.8%
2022	79.3%
2023	84.5%

The above is statistical information on the internet user population in Nigeria from 2017 37.95% to 2020, 65.1% projected to 2023 at 84.5% (Source Statista.com). How you use this information to advance your business is entirely up to you. From the statics above, the internet is undoubted, the present and the future.

Chapter 20
THE RIGHT TIME TO START A BUSINESS

"Sudden and accidental occurrence
Is the limitation of bravery
Yet it is from such unexpected occurrence
That the brave distinguish themselves"

"

In my associations and interaction with people, I have often been presented with such question as:

- When is the right time to start a business?
- How can I identify the business to go into?
- I have a great idea, but I don't have enough funds.
- I think I'm not good enough; entrepreneurs are smarter than I am.
- I want to go into entrepreneurship, but how about my steady job?
- What if the business doesn't work?
- I would have loved to, but my friends all make fun of my idea.
- I have the skill, but how can I push my idea to the public?
- Where do I start?

Although answers to most of the above questions had already been addressed in earlier chapters, some of these questions are borne out of fear and cannot be wished away. The questions, although different, are related. Among them is the preconceived notion that without funds, you cannot start your business. This notion has continued to cause many, even those with bright ideas, to allow such ideas lie fallow until their brilliant idea becomes obsolete. They kept going through their ideas over time until they realize another person has established that same project. Others ask that question because they think they cannot generate business ideas, attract capital, and at other times it is fear of uncertainty.

The Bias of Funds

Some say it is only when they are more comfortable with loads of money to pay the bills and carry other overhead costs to go into business. Of course, the fund is very important in business. Still, you can start a business when you do not have all the needed cash. Most street entrepreneurs started with less or no cash.

It helps to start small and grow the business over time. That way, it reduces mistakes, failures are minimal and not exceptionally devastating should it occur, compared to the shock associated with losing bigger start-up capital.

Although big money, when starting, has advantages, like other things in life, the difference lies in the individual holding the capital and how it is invested. Amounts of start-up capital are not always the issue. It is better to have a good business idea first and then work to make it happen.

A viable idea is like a seed; you only need a good seed and good ground to plant it. After that water, it and nature do the rest while it is in the soil. The job begins at the time of germination; you may choose to tender it in the same place or transplant to another location you think better. Planting is the first stage, after which you pay diligent attention, providing manure until it is nurtured to maturity and harvest.

Business starts with an idea, which is the first step before funding. A great idea attracts people, investors, and supporters who sort after it. Then work and pay attention to details as you support the business to maturity.

The fund is important, but a great idea is far more important than a fund. Ideas attract investors who come with the needed funds. First, identify, create, and develop a feasible and sustainable idea.

If you lack funds, produce a business plan, and look for investors who, through the feasibility of such a business plan, may be convinced to make a commitment and invest in your business.

There are lots of books on how to write a comprehensive winning business plan. Take advantage of loads of information offered through the internet and bring your dream to reality.

The right time to start a business

There is neither the right time nor the right age to start a business. However, there are better periods or less favorable seasons, depending on the nature of the business.

Business can be started at any age or time. Surprisingly, in the U.S., most businesses are started by older people. About 51% of small businesses in that country are started by people aged between 50 - 88years old.

Invariably, 33% are between 35 – 49years old, while 16% are 35 years of age and below. It is important to have a great idea you are passionate about and willing to devote time to make it happen. This involves investing your time, acquiring more knowledge and skill to make that great idea work. It also means depriving yourself of immediate luxury to make such an idea come to life. An ability to make choices and decisions based on one's confidence and convictions are important.

More Considerations before making a business decision:
- The political climate and government policies
- Security of your business location
- Availability of a product or raw materials (depending on the nature of your business) and your targeted market
- Marketing, distribution and sales potentials
- Your skill and knowledge of the business you intend to start
- Knowledge of your competitors is an advantage, and a good mental attitude improves the overall rate of success.

With easier and cheaper, and affordable internet accessibility, you can improve skills, knowledge, and learn globally best practices within any business line.

You can start a business anytime during winter, summer, autumn, harmattan, rainy season, or dry season. It may be any time of the day, month, or year. Business can take off from your home; in the boot of your car, in the Neighborhood Park or garden. What is more important is an idea that can be sustained. A great idea goes with enduring motivation.

The clouds often give way to sunshine.

Some situations inadvertently present opportunities to compel one to start a business and, by extension, a new life. Some opportunities come in rusty, unattractive, and rough packages that it takes inner eyes and perception to identify them.

Sometimes life has a way of tossing people up and down until they discover their directions.

It may be when one has lost that super job: the envy of friends, relatives, and colleagues. It may be the loss of that job you think to have labored for, worked hard, invested your time, energy, a job your life seems to receive its glow and shine from.

Life sometimes does not always give what we desire; neither does it always usher our expectations based on merit. It doesn't always have to follow trends. Often results are obtained by resilience, focus, and share doggedness.

Such a rough time in life can present an opportunity to launch into business, try different hobbies, or acquire new skill sets that enable diversification! Yes, you may need to reprogram and reposition your lifestyle to accommodate new plans, new challenges, new options, and ideas.

Disappointment or loss might provide the opportunity and motivation of a lifetime to start your own business.

When Ken, the senior marketing manager of a small firm, was fired from his job, his sack's terms left a bitter taste behind. Ken was fired after five years of consistently good performance. He was fired and replaced when he couldn't reach and surpass his target for the first and only time in over five years. He thought his past performances should have offered the opportunity for a second chance. He felt used and unappreciated.

After weeks of brooding and self-pity, Ken gathered himself and decided to start his own parallel business in the same city. He hoped to prove his bosses' wrong and eats their words that his glory days were not yet over. Making them eat their words was the motivation he needed to excel.

He worked harder, day and night, traveled places with his crack team of dedicated employees. In about two years, his sales volumes equaled that of his former employers! This was a great fit considering the resources, goodwill, and financial backing of his former employers.

This can also be noticed in football when a player is sold to another club; such a player sometimes starts playing better and even scoring against his former club.

This often happens when terms of the departure did not go down well with the player. At other times it may be because the player wants to prove to his new club that he was sold not because he was not good enough but as a result of non-football issues or other reasons other than performance.

We have seen players who were motivated to succeed as their careers rejuvenated. They increase their tempo in a bid to reward a coach that came to their rescue when their career was taking a downward turn.

For example, a player like Van Parse was sold from Arsenal to Manchester United. In Manchester, Van Parse kept scoring against Arsenal, his former club, whenever both clubs met. At the end of the season, his goals and contributions helped Manchester United win the Premier League in his first season at Manchester United.

Consider also Chelsea goal Keeper Thibaut Courtois when he was sent on loan to Atletico Madrid. At Atletico, Courtois performed exceptionally, making almost impossible saves against his parent club, thereby helping to knock Chelsea out of the Champions League during the semifinal at Stanford Bridge! Thibaut went ahead to help Athletico win the La Liga and qualify them for the Champions League final. Real Madrid went on to win through a classic comeback at additional minutes.

For Van Parse and Thibaut Courtois, their exploit and bravery might result from their loyalty to their various Clubs, that is, loyalty to Manchester United and Athletico Madrid. It may also help prove a point to their former club (Arsenal) or parent club (Chelsea).

The above is something that Italians refer to as the immutable Law of the Ex.

The law of Ex has it that when employees leave one company to a competitor due to disaffection or anger, they tend to perform superiorly at the recipient company.

This happens especially when they are directly faced with the donor company in the competition.[27]

Ken, Thibaut Courtois, and van Parse both found different motivations to excel against their former employers.

Ken's motivation may be out of vendetta and revenge, while Van Persie's may be out of loyalty to Manchester united. This exploits maybe because he knows the strength, weakness, skills, mindset of his former teammates, and his former coach's strategies or tactics (Arsene Wenger). At the same time, in the case of Thibaut Courtois, he may have found a way to show loyalty to Athletico for the confidence they have in him and also make his parent club

---

[27] https://www.execrank.com/board-of-directors-articles/implications-for-people-managers-the-law-of-the-immutable-ex

Chelsea regret keeping him on three years extended loan at Athletico Madrid instead of bringing him back to his parent club. At Athletico Madrid, these exploits earned Thibaut Courtois the first-team recall to Chelsea, his parent club, and guarantee him the first-choice goalkeeper. The immutable law of the Ex-works on occasions!

Business can be started with little resources or nothing but an idea that drives and keeps such alive. These ideas sometimes seem to possess and motivate the individual, keeping them sleepless and restless. Sometimes, it seems the universe conspires to deliver opportunities.

There is a need to know that the excitements and drive in a good idea often beget opportunities.

The problem of lost opportunities is often an insistence on the selfish way of business formation. An example is the 'Chagri and son Ltd' way of doing business. Business owners strongly believed in their ideas or product they choose, not to bring investors or partners. As a result, they kept struggling with avoidable limitations just because they want the business. They expected profit to remain in the family.

The business has evolved and developed above the stage. It must remain in the family, where family members alone head departments even where more competent people can do the job outside. In such cases, you see the business struggling because the owner refuses to invite the best hands to either invest in the business or refuse to let go of management and control sensitive positions to more competent hands, not family members. Examples abound in recent times when a family member ran down a huge conglomerate, where its competitor later acquired the firm. This is because the founder wanted the leadership to remain in the family through inexperienced and incapable hands.

The business performs better when additional best hands are allowed to invest, manage, and bring their expertise into the business.

Do you possess the necessary skills, experience, time, and resources to set your idea rolling? This is very important as there are two issues here, having a brilliant idea and having the requisite knowledge, skill, or resources to make it workable and profitable.

A team of qualified professionals will work wonders close to a miracle in kick-starting the business compared to when you go it alone. Remember the old saying; two (good) heads are better than one.

Usually, better-qualified individuals are a little expensive to hire at an earlier stage. The better option will invite them to invest or partner in your great idea while retaining the business's higher percentage share value.

I have seen a lot of businessmen who eventually make big profits in their businesses. Instead of coming up with better long term plans for their business sustenance, they often make wrong choices that dealt mortal blows to the thriving young business.

Many of these prospective businesses collapsed before they had time to thrive. If they had invested wisely, the business would be active and vibrant.

Nature itself supports gradual and steady growth, but a man in his quick-fix ways introduced faster and quicker growths that sometimes leave much to be desired while it has its benefits. Whenever we alter the natural order, something adverse seems to result. Consequently, we either go the extra miles to fix or result in problems that are often managed with no lasting solution.

Consistency and Continuity always make a difference!

Young business owners should rejoice that they can afford that luxury item or other want yet have the patience to defer gratification, grow their business, and make both short and long-term plans. Knowing that later they can gradually acquire those things they desired without mortgaging their business's life to unhealthy, avoidable, and damaging lifestyles.

Generating winning business ideas

Many questions come to bear in my dealings with young people concerning generating ideas and starting a business. Some of such questions are sincere and honest questions aimed at knowing and learning the right way to do things and avoid pitfalls. It is also a result of challenges in generating winning business ideas or outright fear of failure or making mistakes.

Such questions include, how do I identify the business to run? What kind of business should I run? When and how can I run my business and many such related questions?

The age-long rule has been to find a need, provide solutions, look for one that is not appropriately run and run it better. These cliché and mantra served people in the past and still serves to date. The problem is that people often go out searching for that space as if they are searching for a lost item. Others go searching as one that walks into a supermarket to enquire where a particular product line is located within the supermarket. Either way, it won't be easy to find your ideal business immediately.

When there were practically only one company producing nodules in Nigeria with little or no competition, many guys in the street knew that they would make a huge profit if they provide an alternative. And even much profit when they provide a better alternative. But there were many hindrances against setting up their own noodle business as such industries may be capital intensive.

Today, several industries produce nodules. These new industries have taken a large chunk of the market previously held by one company. To keep hold of the larger market, you see the companies coming up with new products that offer the consumers varieties. They also engage in extensive marketing to bring their products as close as possible to their consumers irrespective of their place aboard.

However, you may not necessarily go for a capital intensive business as a start-up with very little or no fund. You can start small with what you have and where you are.

You do not need to go searching for a need to fill. The senses must be active and alert to identify opportunities wherever and whenever it shows up, which is the hallmark of entrepreneurship.

Everyone can develop the senses to achieve whatever they set their mind on. It begins with being alert to environments around you.

Please do not ignore the power of Brainstorming; it leads to purposeful insight. You can develop your hobbies and turn them into great business ideas.

Be open to ideas and find ways to make already existing things better; this is called innovation. Always be attentive to the need of your environment. And then raise a business plan to gauge your idea.

A business plan does not necessarily aim to raise money for your business; of course, that is part of the aim. Assuredly, a Business plan also helps to identify the product or service that is viable and appropriate. It then offers strategies to achieve that goal. It shows your strength, expected challenges, and future projections in the market. It immensely helps to access what you have at hand to start; these include your financial strength and, of course, your competitors. It gives an overview of the intended business. By it, you are equipped to meet and mitigate difficulties that may come up later.

Made strong in broken places

We can be made strong in broken places. An obstacle can be turned into opportunities. For example, the footballer Kanu Nwankwo; when he was diagnosed with a heart condition, it could have meant the end of a fledgling career. Still, he continued playing after successful heart surgery but went ahead to win additional trophies.

Today that terrible experience led to his establishing Kanu Heart Foundation. This foundation has saved the lives of many kids with heart diseases.

Our problems can provide an opportunity to excel. Yes, we can be made strong, even stronger, in broken places.

What is the need of the community and neighborhood where you live or work? It all starts by being observant of things happening around you.

Perhaps there are no restaurants, especially on weekends, and the bachelors and young ladies are having it tough on weekends. Can you provide an affordable weekend catering service or restaurant with excellent service? It can be a weekend home delivery business.

Are there things you believe are not properly done that you would have wanted it done better? It may be the need for a more decent or professionally run viewing center that provides snacks and drinks. It could be an inefficient gardener yet charges exorbitantly. Can you provide a better alternative? It may be that people in your neighborhood or social circle complain over the lack of plumbers, electricians, people to mow their lawn. It could be an environmental threat posed by non-degradable nylon sachet and plastic water bottles littering everywhere from the supermarkets and grocery shops. It may be a need for good auto-mechanics to solve car owners' plight due to the explosion of unqualified auto mechanics.

Your environmental need may present an urgent opportunity to introduce paper bags that are degradable to replace the non-degradable nylon constituting eye sour in your neighborhood. What you do to alleviate these problems in your environment could lead to a new business that solves these problems.

Here is an excerpt on generating ideas from of beautiful new book 'The Entrepreneur Code' [28]

Generating ideas –useful ideas- is a skill. Like other skills, it can be learned; the more you practice, the easier it will be to develop ideas whenever needed.

Unique ideas are the bedrock of great businesses; generating the business idea right for you is the first hurdle every entrepreneur must cross. It must not be original but unique.

Let's explore ways to generate business ideas;

Keep your eyes open

Seek for things that capture your attention and interests, ask yourself questions about it, and narrow your focus to zero in on the idea.

Examine an old mousetrap...then build a better one

Deliberately analyze products and services that don't meet your high standards and create a better product, service, or experience.

Take it to the streets.

Great ideas can always be discovered by navigating the neighborhoods for trends, fads, street cultures, sports, and general people's interest.

Tap your interests

---

[28] *The Entrepreneur Code: Inspiring Another generation of Afropreneurs*

Thousands of clever entrepreneurs just took up their hobbies and turned them into very successful businesses; you too can. Take time out to study your interests. Do you enjoy browsing, hanging out on social media, painting, writing, washing? Do you love fashion passionately? Why don't you sit down and develop a business idea around that? Many have done it.

Look at things that bug you.

This may not sound very profound but think of a list of things that annoys you, which you wished were different and begin to imagine the solutions that will make them better. This has been a huge source of ideas that changed the entrepreneurial world.

King C. Gillette was fed up with the tedious process of sharpening his straight-edge razor and founded the massive disposable razor industry.

If you hate long queues, shabby customer services, poor delivery services, long wait for taxis and buses, dirty estates, you name it; these are clues to businesses that can solve them all. It's up to you.

Travel

Move to a new location; your eyes will be open to many opportunities and potential business ideas that will shock you. Leopoldo Fernandez Pujas of TelePizza, one of Spain's leading Fast-food companies, got the idea from Domino Pizza during his visit to the United States today; his company grosses over $250m in sales annually with over 13,000 employees in 8 countries.

Sleep on it

Just before going to bed, think about the ideas you want to generate. Get specific; "I will come up with new ways of promoting our new product" keep a pen and note pad handy to capture the ideas as soon as you wake up.

Many great ideas have emanated from sleep, many times; they come as strange, unintelligible stuff…my advice, don't ignore your dreams and quickly jot them down before you forget them.

Meditations

The everyday hustling and bustling naturally crowd out our minds with concerns, urgent deadlines, stress, and challenges.

Clear your mind through quiet meditations, quietly focus on your future, on solving a problem, providing a solution, or creating a product, do this continuously for hours weekly, and sooner than later; you'll make that discovery. It works!

Engage your brain through structured exercises

Get a partner, take 10 minutes (timed) to come up with 40 ideas on a specific subject or challenge, you may not get the whole, but you will discover the strength of your brain to your amazements. This requires the commitment of time and energy. Your brain needs time and space to function optimally; engage it regularly.

Curiosity

This is the foundation of creativity; in today's world, thinking outside the box is noble and respected. We value innovation's power, but all these proceeds from curiosity- from asking, looking, and observing.

Scanning our environment, engaging, and exercising our minds is critical to developing superlative and great ideas; in the words of Socrates…" wisdom begins in wonder."

Go Online

Look up entrepreneurship and industry-related communities. Go to Twitter and search relevant hashtags to see what is trending. For example, if you have interests in social finance and social innovation, consider hashtags like #impinv (impact investing), #socfin (Social Finance), #socent (Social Entrepreneur or Social Enterprise).

Do random web surfing sometimes; virtually every search engine has a 'What's New' and 'What's Hot' section, where you will find new trends, news tidbits, and hot new websites; these may trigger an idea or concept you never thought of.

Get an outsider's opinion.

Bringing in a fresh perspective can make all the difference. Ask someone who is not familiar with your situation or environment. It could be a friend, spouse, a relative abroad, or a colleague. They may just provide the missing link to an idea you overlooked because it probably was too obvious or due to familiarity.

Listen

Your customers can give you ideas for your new product or solutions or improve the current ones that can open up new markets for you.

Change Your Routine

New surroundings and new experiences can stimulate your brain and get you thinking differently.

Drive a new route to the office, try new restaurants, work in a different area, and visit a place you've always ignored.

Watch Television programs and series you ordinarily don't like watching, play new games, just break away from your routine.

Read New Books

Read something new; business books, magazines, blogs. The more you load yourself with new things, the more likely you will develop the capacity to put together seemingly unrelated concepts to create something new.

Validating your Idea!

Your IDEA is guilty until proven innocent and has generated great ideas; you must test and validate them before you start investing your time and resources into it.

They must be proven "innocent" through a painstaking testing and validating exercise.

One of the biggest mistakes of entrepreneurs the world over are falling so much in love with their ideas that they inadvertently refuse to see very obvious flaws.

Businesses are established, and Jobs created when you provide solutions to the problems around you. You must be observant of the needs of your environment. Identify these needs. Think of the immediate, then future need of your community and begin planning today. The problems around you may provide creativity and self-empowerment opportunities when you have provided answers and solutions to these challenges. Think ahead!

PART FOUR

NEED WE REST ON OUR OARS?

OUR WORLD IS CHANGING

As global citizens of a fast-paced changing world, a digital generation where we seem to live our lives online through the internet, we must work and do our parts in our little ways to prepare for tomorrow's needs. A tomorrow we may or may not be part of.

This generation got to where we are at the moment because others somewhere, sometime in the distant past, made an effort that that has brought unimaginable benefits for us today. While many civilized societies have vigorously improved the standard of living for its citizens, many other regions still battle the scourge of poverty, with millions of their citizens living below the poverty line. What this means is that all hands must be on deck to bring solutions to this menace. The cardinal solution, as noted in previous chapters, remains job creation. It is generally agreed that government alone cannot bring the needed solution to eradicate unemployment worldwide.

Small business and entrepreneurship will help provide the leverage needed to defeat the global unemployment crisis. Yet, it is difficult for entrepreneurs to thrive in an unstable environment.

Inexperience, lack of skills and needed knowledge, ignorance, corruption, and unfriendly government policies pose obstacles that reduce success and hinder economic growth.

There is a need to start from where we are and with what is available. That is the essence of street entrepreneurs. We do not have to lose faith as a result of the challenges of the time. The Great depression was surmounted; the 2008 financial crisis was conquered. 911 brought its lessons, and the solution drive engages. Covid -19 will be surmounted, and a new set of street preneurs will be unleashed as an outcome of that pandemic. Surmounting these challenges means creating a solution to the myriads of problems and bringing innovation into such solutions. When we get a solution to the problems staring us in the face, we are at that moment creating jobs and unleashing our entrepreneurial capabilities. Our input today determines tomorrow's outcome. The implication is that no matter the challenges or the height of our achievements, we mustn't rest on our oars!

Chapter 21
WHEN THE ACCOUNT CAN'T FLY

…we need no mourners in our stride
No remorse, no tears
Only this resolve
That the locust shall never again
Visit our farmstead
-Odia Ofeimum.

It was a bright Saturday morning in October 2008. I had earlier stopped at a bank to make a transfer on my way to a program. I had barely entered the auditorium when my phone started vibrating; I took my seat then removed my phone from my pocket to have a look. I was amazed by the text message from a bank I do not have an account.

Curiosity got the better of me. I decided to read through the message, thinking this must be a mistake, but how could a bank I do not operate have my name and account number and even ask me to come immediately.

I was in Kaduna that weekend for a wedding; a friend who traveled got financially stranded in a distant state. He sent his account details; I walked into the bank to pay money into his bank account when the double honk of a car horn caught my attention. It was an old school mate; although we lived and worked in the same city, we had not seen for nearly three years. He stopped, parked, and got out as we exchanged pleasantries. Once we were done, I entered the bank premises. I did not notice that there were two different banks in the mall beside each other.

The banking hall was barely busy that Saturday morning and the teller guys were in a good mood. We chatted as if we knew each other though that was my first time in that bank branch. I filled out the details; even though I was at the wrong bank, the account number fitted the spaces provided. I later left with the instruction that they should make the transfer immediately. I had rushed out of the bank and straight to the program and barely sat down when the text message came into my phone.

"Very urgent Chris, please come to the bank now, your account can't fly, the account number is wrong. Please respond fast. Thanks".

I had gone to the wrong bank with the correct account details belonging to another bank. No matter how this bank tried, even when the numbers fitted the spaces, the account can't just fly. It does not matter if they use the best IT professional or the best software engineer. This is a case of a round peg in a square hole.

I then realize the mistake when I got to the bank as I now saw the bank's name written boldly, and just beside it was the bank I was to have made the transfer. I had wrongly assumed that it was just one bank on the premises.

I took the deposit slip, told the teller the mistake tore it to shreds and immediately entered the bank I was meant to be, made the transfer, and within seconds the transfer went through.

If we had persisted, to make the account go through, I would still have been there to this day struggling, frustrated, and determined to make progress that never will be.

This is what happens in business and life, generally. Some people cannot accept that 'this- account- can't- just- fly' no matter the energy they exert in it.

They give in everything they have, flogging a dead horse and expecting a response. They strategize and re-strategize as they put more hours in perseverance, hoping for an opening that will never come.

But you are in the wrong project with the right plan and right strategy; the account can't just fly. It is time to bring sunset to that project no matter the effort that has been committed.

Not long ago, I met a lady sitting for joint admission and matriculation board(JAMB) exam for the past ten years because she prefers to study a particular course and a specific university.

She was on the verge of giving up education entirely when I met her. She did not pick the current University JAMB form, which has already closed till the next year.

She even made a joke that "she hope to chat a new cause, get married sooner and take whatever life dishes her after all, she had giving her best and it did not work out perhaps that is her destiny."

I was able to convince her to try other universities. I may try another course while concentrating in her catchment area. This is the height of routinely doing the wrong thing for a very long time and blaming destiny for failure.

We are created intelligent beings and have the capacity to gather information, analyze the situation, and draw conclusions. We should be able to sit down at times and ask ourselves such simple questions as;

Why is this not just working?

Is there something I have been doing wrong? Do I need advice or opinion from experienced people or professionals?

Why should we go through years suffering avoidable disappointment, stubbornly refusing to see reasons and accept the right answers even when the evidence is overwhelming and compelling?

Sometimes it is obvious that you are in the wrong location, and yet you want to eke out gold where it never exists. It can be exhausting, time-wasting, and draining working in futility.

You float a business where there is high overhead, and you end up winding down such business after years of running the outfit with little or no profit.

The problem may be funding, packaging, location, or family demand, which is more than income. Identify the problem and address it before you get your turn around.

You cannot have an appointment in the east while driving towards the west. Even though the earth is spherical, you would have been old and dying before getting close to your destination.

A journey of a thousand kilometers ends up taking a lifetime, yet the destination was not reached. How exhausting, painful, and worthless the trip!

It does not matter how hard you hit the nail or how long you stay hitting it. As far as there is obstruction tougher than the nail, the nail will not penetrate an inch further. If you persist and apply further force to drive in the nail, you'll realize that even metals do bend or break; either way, it's a fruitless effort.

An entrepreneur must be bold enough to know when to seek help, merge with others, sell or leave a particular business or location.

Sometimes people are so committed to an idea, a plan, or a dream. They rarely see reality even when the evidence is overwhelming that the idea couldn't fly. When plans are not going as planned despite efforts, it is wise to seek council from external experienced and trusted avenues.

Business failure is not the end of the world. No one is immune to it. It could happen even to the most experience of businessmen.

The difference is that such a person knows how to keep moving; they know when, despite losing capital, they know when to let go and start afresh. If not for anything, they must have learned better ways to handle such mistakes that led to the business's collapse in the first place.

There is nothing like a total failure in business. You may have lost the capital, but something must have been gained. It is possible that in pursuit of your interest, you may discover something else.

In his Book, the Philosophy of History, George W Friedrich Hegel wrote, "what is involved here is in world history something else results from the actions of Men than they intend and achieves, something else than what they know or want. They accomplish their interest but something else is accomplished which was implied in it, but which was not in the conscience and intention of the actors."

A friend went for a business trip that didn't go as he had expected, but while there, he met a lady who later became the love of his life and eventually his wife.

There are footballers, coaches, politicians, and businessmen who have written bestselling books to document the successes, failures, and experiences gathered in their career paths.

Nelson Mandela wrote about his experience at Robben Island, a prisoner for about 18years of his 27 prison years; the book sold the world.

Many businessmen start running training, workshop, and consultancy for entrepreneurs. These businesspeople share their experiences, including their failures and success stories, to help start-ups, corporations, and other business people avoid such pitfalls that would have been damaging to them and their corporation, thereby increasing productivity.

John Shephard Baron, the man who invented the first ATM cash machine, came up with the concept of self-service cash dispenser in 1965 while lying in a bath after getting to his bank too late to withdraw money. Hear John Shepherd – Baron speak.

"I remember back in 1965 that I would always take money out of my bank on a Saturday morning. However, one Saturday, I was one minute late at my bank, and it was closed. "That night, I started thinking that there must be a better way to get cash when I wanted it. I thought of the chocolate vending machine, where money was put in a slot, and a bar dispatched, surely money could be dispensed in the same way"[29]. .

From the circumstance above, we see disappointment leading to invention. Instead of whining about how you had a bad day, a bad investment, think productively; something good can still result from a bad situation.

It is good to read the success stories of entrepreneurs. Still, it is even better to read accounts of failed businesses and why they failed. There is no total failure; the lessons in the failures may be the reasons for the tremendous successes afterward.

In 1754, Horace Walpole, a politician, and writer coined the word 'Serendipity' from the Persian fairy tale 'The Three Princes of Serendip.' The Heroes were always making discoveries, by accidents and sagacity of things they were not in quest of.

Today in our dictionaries, Serendipity has come to mean 'The occurrence and developments of events by chance happily or beneficially, a pleasant surprise or happy accident.

The popular antibiotic, Penicillin was discovered by accident; in 1928, Alexander Flaming, as the story goes, had embarked on vacation and forgot to wash the dish in his laboratory before going on the trip.

On his return Alexander observed molds growing on the staphylococci bacteria in the unwashed dish, but that was not all; he also discovered that the molds killed the bacteria, which was the birth of a groundbreaking discovery –Penicillin. An antibiotic that has saved millions of lives around the globe was a product discovered by accident!

In business and life generally, train your eyes, mind, and imagination to identify lessons from situations and bring new development. Such development can undergo more improvement for a better outcome.

Failure may be that turnaround ingredient needed to get positioned for a better future.

We can learn to sometimes corporate with the inevitable chaos and strive to turn them into orderliness and opportunities.

Laced in that veil of difficulty and discomfort may perhaps be the opportunity for self-discovery and actualization. Sometimes some situations expose and help you identify other opportunities you initially didn't set out.

A transport company later identifies that courier business can go hand in hand and lower operational cost when combined with their original transportation business. It is the same vehicles, airplane, train, or ship in their usual daily routine that will be conveying these couriers with little or no additional cost through their existing routes and destinations. They are helping their clients who want to send couriers and other products without going along with the goods. A courier company was born.

Then in time, the entrepreneur watches his stranded passengers. They have a hard time getting an affordable hotel to pass the night. Sometimes these travelers had to sleep in the terminals till the next day as in cases where meetings, exams, interviews, and programs were rescheduled. Here, the entrepreneur may decide to build affordable low-budget hotel accommodations to alleviate these passengers' problems. The hotel business is born.

With the hotel, business comes catering, Call Centers, Car hire, international language translation Centre and other sub businesses sprouting from the original idea. The list of new sub businesses that came to be but unintended earlier can go on and on. They all started with the transport business.

These were business opportunities identified by accident, opportunities that perhaps were not originally in the entrepreneur's mind when he started the transport business.

Pay attention to these sub businesses that can come up from the original business and give little attention to the critics, who stand judging at your predicament in difficult times. You can, through your failing, fail successfully forward.

Chapter 22

LET'S PLANT TOMORROW

When there is surplus
Even ants benefit from it
Dee moss

SOWING FOR FUTURE GENERATION

Several years ago, my family moved to a bungalow in a quiet neighborhood with many empty lands lying fallow.

The previous tenant, a Ghanaian, had planted flowers, citrus trees, plantain, avocado pear, and left behind a fertile land for a vegetable garden.

When the Ghanaian moved into the estate, there were empty spaces that could be used as a garden, but the tenants in the estate were not interested in any form of gardening, be it crop growing or flower gardening.

He plowed as many portions in the estate's empty land, as it was a government estate with some plots of land yet undeveloped. He was able to claim enough spaces for farming before other tenants decided to join in the rush for a free piece of land to plant vegetables.

In those days, once you selected and cultivate a portion of land, no tenant in the estate will contest it with you. It remained like that for ten years until we moved out just around the same time the Government decided to bring in developers to complete that part of the project.

Apart from the plantains that the Ghanaian may have harvested, he never stayed long enough in Nigeria to enjoy the fruit-bearing trees. He relocated to his country before the fruit trees, which took long years to reach maturity, yielded.

We, the tenants that arrived after he had left, enjoyed these fruits and beautiful flowers planted by a tenant we never knew. We inherited a piece of land and planted vegetables that served almost all our vegetable needs year-round. This former tenant's effort helped my family in a challenging period of economic downturn when we almost relied on the proceeds from the garden to meet the family's nutritional needs.

My family rarely bought plantains all through our stay in that estate as there were enough to harvest from our garden. There was always fruits to pluck at every season of the year. Because of the high yielding quality species of the plantain, other neighbors and family guests often request the plantain sucker for planting. When my parents eventually left that estate, there was a traffic of friends who asked my parents to speak to the landlord on their behalf so they could be the next tenants of bungalow 37B. Thanks to that unknown Ghanaian tenant, whose name only very few tenants in the estate bothered to remember.

I believe that experience contributed and encouraged my parents to plant more fruit trees and flowers wherever we lived. We left every environment better than we met it, whether we were there temporally or not, rented or purchased. This was a lesson I learned while growing up.

The need to be altruistic in life is among the virtues my father extolled and maintained as we developed. He emphasized the need to live an unselfish life that empowered tomorrow is a sure way to personal prosperity and long term success that benefits the community. To him, empowering the future is like a surplus that benefits even ants. This, to him, is continuity.

Do not always seek to reap all you sow, he often advises. Sometimes you sow, and it will be reaped by the coming generation, benefiting them greatly.

Mayor Julian Castro made a statement that buttressed this point in his keynote speech at the 2012 Democratic National Convention of

American election that returned Barack Obama for his second tenure as American President:

"In the end, the American dream is not a sprint, or even a marathon, but a relay. Our families don't always cross the finish line in one generation but each generation passes on to the next generation, the fruit of their labors... my mother fought for civil right so that instead of a mop, I could hold this microphone."

This is part of vision, working for the benefit of both present and future generations.

Any family, organization, or government that aims to grow and maintain growth has to sow both for today and the future, a sustainable growth that outlives the present generation. A short-term plan is as important as the long term, two sides of the same coin. Emphasis on one over the other reduces its power, value, and renders it counterfeit.

Like in construction, you never really stopped building after the house (building) has been erected; as the years go by, you repaint the house. Later, as the years continue to move on, you renovate the structure, and after you may decide to redesign the structure. This is to meet contemporary styles. You may even demolish and start the whole process of building again, perhaps the reason it is called a building!

Some time ago, I saw an article whose author was not mentioned, but 'from archives' the article made so much impression on me because it relates to my childhood experience with the Ghanaian ex-tenant that I preserved the article in my junk box for years.

"Charles Good year, a bankrupt hardware merchant from Philadelphia, USA, discovered the art of vulcanizing (after, the Roman god of fire) rubber in the winter of 1839.

When he died in 1860, he was $200,000 in debt. Neither Good Year nor his family was ever connected with the company named in his honor. Today's billion dollar Good year Tire and Rubber Company, the world's largest rubber business…"

It went on to say that "… today there is a cultivated rubber tree for every two human beings on earth. Millions of milkers harvest the crop. This huge apparatus owes its existence to the invincible little fanatics who might have died a bitter man but didn't.

Charles Goodyear himself wrote that "Life should not be estimated exclusively by the standard of dollars and cents. I am not disposed to complain that I have planted and another has gathered the fruits. A man has cause for regret only when he sows and no one reaps" (from the Archives).

Not long ago, researchers tracked down Jonathan Fletcher, who has now been recognized in some quarters as the 'forgotten Father of The Search Engine.' Granted that there were computers searching before the advent of the web, Jonathan was the first person to create a search engine with all the modern search engine components. As a result, it could be argued that he built the first modern search engine.

Jonathan Fletcher invented the Jump Station, an easy to navigate search tool index over twenty years ago before Google came to be. Yet if you put Jonathan Fletcher's name into Google search, none of the immediate results will show his role in developing the World Wide Web. While Sergey Brim and Larry Page, founders of Google, are household names. There is certainly nothing to credit Mr. Fletcher. Yet twenty years ago, in a computer lab at the University of Sterling Scotland, Mr. Fletcher invented the world's first web crawling search engine, the technology that powers Google, Bing, Yahoo, and all the major search tools on the web today. These current mediums make a lot of money for those who followed after Fletcher, but the Scarborough-born pioneer has no regret.[30] Hear him

---

[30] *Joe Miller. BBC*

"My parents are proud of me, My Children are proud of me
And that's worth quite a lot to me, So I'm happy".
-Jonathan Fletcher

The story of Charles Goodyear, Jonathan Fletcher, and our old garden goes on to illustrate that there are times we may not reap at the moment, the benefits from the fruit of our labor. Such efforts and sacrifice fuel the wheel of progress, which may, in time, be reaped by another or provide a base for further and better inventions.

Where could civilization be today if we strive only to reap all our investment in our lifetime, stopping or keeping on hold those projects that will not mature in our life time?

Many great scientists never lived to see the work they started, which benefited humanity after their demise.

Think of the missionaries' who took religion, education, and medicine to a different remote part of the globe against odds. They put their lives on the front lines, in danger and harm's way, as they voyaged into isolated areas. Today, many medical missionaries still go to the most remote and volatile places on earth to bring health, food, education, religion, and comfort to such dwellers.

On occasion, I hear people say, "why should I plant flowers, trees, fruits and other greenery in a rented apartment where I may not stay to harvest or reap the fruits." Imagine how our world would have been with such an attitude and mindset. It would have resulted in stagnated civilization and a dearth of inventions.

Our world is better for it today due to investments made in past research. Yet, the inventors embraced it with all zealousness to bequeath to generation next, as a pedestal to proceed.

Most advanced technologies we enjoy today are either improved from past effort and prototype or gained its major idea from already existing blueprints. Some of our research, educational ,scholarships, grants, and other foundations that have benefitted this era are products of endowments created by people from past generations, helping to create a better future that they knew they would not witness. Mankind's greatest successes and achievements are based on the ability to think and plan ahead of time.

There are more private Philanthropic foundations (past and present) whose benefits bring about Global development across locations and fields. Some of these foundations have far-reaching benefits across cities, countries, and continents. They will continue to benefit many who may never know the individuals or organizations behind its establishment. Examples of such private foundations include:

Bill & Melinda Gates Foundation

Established by Microsoft founder Bill Gates, his wife Melinda and father William H. Gates Sr. in 1994, the Gates Foundation claims the largest charitable endowment globally. It supports development and health programs in more than 100 countries. The foundation's ambitious platform for agricultural development aims to "help 150 million of the world's poorest farming families in Sub-Saharan Africa and South Asia lift themselves out of extreme poverty by 2025."

Ford Foundation

The Ford Foundation began with a $25,000 gift from Edsel Ford, son of Ford Motor Co. founder Henry Ford, in 1936. Today, with over 44,000 proposals received each year, it has become one of the world's largest philanthropies, with grants given to projects and individuals in more than 50 countries in Latin America, Africa, and Asia. The foundation's nine focus areas are democratic and accountable governance, economic fairness, educational opportunity and scholarship, freedom of expression, human rights, metropolitan opportunity, sexuality and reproductive health and rights, social justice philanthropy, and sustainable development. The organization's "Strengthening Human Rights Worldwide" establishes it as a global program seeking to strengthen institutions in enforcing human rights laws and standards[31].

Children's Investment Fund Foundation(CLIFF)

CIFF was established in 2002 by hedge fund manager Chris Hohn and his wife, Jamie. Its current focus areas are child survival, hunger alleviation, and educational achievement. With laser-sharp focus, CIFF concentrates on just 15 to 20 projects annually, all having a demonstrable, large-scale impact on children's lives. Future core areas and funding opportunities are adolescent reproductive health, early childhood development, economic readiness, and care environment. CIFF's international programs in Africa, particularly Angola, Benin, Botswana, Burkina Faso, Burundi, Côte d'Ivoire, and Cameroon, are focused on medical care and educational support for children with HIV, aimed at reducing maternal and child mortality, and initiating post-conflict reintegration programs for children. In Asia, the foundation aims to improve access to education and boost treatment for HIV/AIDS.[32]

Open Society Foundations

Founded by investor and philanthropist George Soros in 1984, Open Society Foundations were initially designed to help countries transition from communism to democracy. Today, Open Society focuses on establishing democracy through programs that advance good governance, justice, education, public health, and independent media in more than 70 countries in Europe, Asia, Africa, and Latin America. Funding for media and arts programs that help facilitate government transparency and accountability,

---

[31] Noel Salazar (https://www.devex.com/news/top-10-philanthropic-foundations-a-primer-75508).

[32] www.devex.com /en/organizations/ciff

women's rights, and migrant equality are expected to figure strongly in Open Society's future plans.[33]

William and Flora Hewlett Foundation

The William and Flora Hewlett Foundation funds global development programs on governance, education, improved policy analysis, and better access to agricultural markets for farmers in developing countries. Initiatives on energy efficiency and renewable energy are expected to take center stage as the foundation expands its environment and energy portfolio.[34]

United Nations Foundation

In 1998, media mogul Ted Turner gifted the United Nations with $1 billion for disbursement within 10 years. This historic pledge created the United Nations Foundation. This organization encourages wealthy countries, individuals, and groups to contribute to and support the United Nations' development and peacekeeping efforts. The foundation gives its entire revenue to global development, focusing on child health, climate change, peace and security, and poverty eradication. Its future endeavors are expected to center on women's health, the plight of women and girls in developing countries, and the elimination of preventable diseases such as measles, malaria, and polio in the developing world.[35]

John D. and Catherine T. MacArthur Foundation

In 1978, business giant John MacArthur's estate started one of the largest private foundations in the United States. Its international programs focus on human rights and international justice, peace and security, conservation and sustainable development, higher education in Africa and Russia, migration and human mobility, and population and reproductive health[36].

---

[33] www.soros.org/
[34] www.heweltt.org/
[35] www.devex.com/en/organizations/un-foundation

Rockefeller Foundation

When the Rockefeller Foundation's board of trustees appropriated $25,000 to create the International Health Commission in 1913, it set the stage for philanthropy's role in global development. Today, the organization's focus areas are international in scope: basic survival safeguards, global health, climate and environment, urbanization, and social and economic security. With the creation of the Asian Cities Climate Change Resilience Network in 2009, funding for environment-related projects, particularly those focused on mitigating the effects of climate change, is expected to rise. Global health programs will continue to receive strong support and agricultural development initiatives in honor of the late Nobel laureate Norman Borlaug, a pioneering agronomist, and long-time foundation partner.[37]

Tony Elumelu Foundation (TEF) Chairman, Heirs Holdings

Having seen how a $5million investment in a small, dying bank about two decades ago transformed it into a respected global brand, Tony Elumelu, the former CEO of UBA, now inspires young generations of African entrepreneurs to actively play greater roles in the development of the continent.

His reach-out channel is the Tony Elumelu Foundation (TEF), which focuses on supporting entrepreneurs in Africa by enhancing the competitiveness of the private sector; and built on a vision it terms 'Africapitalism.'

Elumelu often cites the UBA example, which he helped build into a multinational, pan-African financial institution that has created 25,000 jobs, generated wealth in communities all across Africa, expanded finance for trade, created stronger financial infrastructure for investment and economic growth, paid taxes to national and

---

[36] www.macfound.org/
[37] www.rockefellerfoundation.org/

local governments to support public services, and given millions of customers control over their financial lives.

The foundation's goal is to help grow 1000, leading African SMEs into a pan-African and global business that employ significant numbers, pay taxes, and create prosperity and wealth.

"We also plan to build a world-class business school in Nigeria in the long-term," adds Elumelu, also the Chairman of Heirs Holdings, which has significant interests in the ICT, financial services, energy, real estate and hospitality, agribusiness, and healthcare sectors. TEF supports projects like the Nigeria Fast Growth 50 to demonstrate our desire to embrace global opportunities and practices while ensuring that as much as possible of the value-adding aspects of Africa's resource wealth stay on the African continent.

"It is my hope that the foundation will inspire business and entrepreneurs to actively play more role in Africa's development. This is my vision of 'Africapitalism,'" Elumelu concludes.[38] [39]

Rose of Sharon Foundation (ROSF)

Being a woman herself, Folorunso Alakija's philanthropic gestures are naturally targeted primarily at women and young people. Her vehicle of charity is the Rose of Sharon Foundation (ROSF). The main objective includes easing the burdens of existence for widows and orphans through community networks.

Alakija, the CEO of the Rose of Sharon Group, has helped to fend for widows, widows' children and see orphans through university through her foundation.

[38] http://www.nairaland.com/1944436/top-5-nigerian-philanthropists-inspiring
[39] Mfong Obong Nsehe (http://www.forbes.com/sites/mfonobongnsehe/2013/01/20/the-most-generous-philanthropists-in-africa-in-2012/#3dd5735076a3)

The former banking executive-turned-fashion designer-turned oil magnate says her organization's next goal is to help set up schools across Nigeria, in areas where the women would work the land. At the same time, their children would attend classes within walking distance.

DOING YOUR PART

Our generation will make giant strides if everyone does their parts in any chosen endeavor, career, and pursuit they find interest in. With a huge youth population, the youth in Nigeria would have successfully determined the direction of the economy and leadership.

Doing your part infers that you should do all within your power to excel in whatever venture or endeavor you find yourself; by investing more time, making commitment and sacrifice, finding reasons to motivate yourself after each disappointment, and striving to accomplish a task even when you feel like caving in.

Doing your part also involves taking responsibility for your action or inaction and not complaining about how things should have been done better. This is aptly captured in the words of President Theodore Roosevelt of the USA.

" It is not the critic who counts, not the man who points out how the strong man stumbled or where the doer of deeds could have done them better, the credit belongs to the man who is actually in the arena, who strives valiantly, who errs and comes short again and again, who knows the great enthusiasms, the great devotions, who spends himself in a worthy cause, who at the best knows in the end the triumph of high achievement, and who, at worst, if he fails, at least fails while daring greatly, so that his place shall never be with those timid souls who knows neither victory nor defeat."

The Millenials, new Generation of young adults and the entire citizenry must work together to ensure the kind of life and business they deserve. Your destiny is in your hands has become an appealing lyric that is hardly acted upon in reality. Going forward each individual must provide the needed motivation to excel against odds.

It is excellent to be an A student, but you must not necessarily have A's in every course of study to succeed.

Consider a student who is not too good in chemistry but excellent in Physics. Doing your part means that you should not give up on chemistry because of the difficulty in getting excellent grades as you do in physics. It means you invest more time in chemistry or at least an equal amount of time that you invest in Physics. It means you study any material available to you in chemistry. Just Do Your Part! Then after you have given your best shot, be bold to accept whatever turns up fair and square, but experience shows that quite often, you come up with your head held high.

Professor William James, a Harvard Psychologist, wrote.

"Let no youth have any anxiety about the upshot of his education whatever the line it may be. If he keeps faithfully busy each hour of the working day, he may safely leave the final result to itself. He can with perfect certainty count on waking some time to find himself one of the competent ones of his generation in whatever pursuit he may have singled out".

Some failed to do their part because others are not doing theirs or because the odds are high and seem against them. Others fail to do their part because it looks foolish in others'others' eyes even when they are convinced it is their best option. They will eventually snuff out and suffocate the greatness in them.

When you fail to do your part because others are not doing theirs, that which you have will continue to diminish until, like an unattended bent candle, it burns itself out prematurely faster and wasted.

Doing your part can be rewarding. It's like taking the initiative, going the extra mile, and making the right decision without been told. It gains you unsolicited positive attention and promotions. It helps you excel.

Still using the academic example, you may be a student with an A in Biology and C in Agriculture. The A in Biology might be your strength. You need to specialize in occasionally taping from your C in Agriculture to be a genius in Biology!

It is also possible that your physical frailty will not allow you to excel with the pressure or demand related to carpentry or auto mechanics, even when you know you could do well in both. You may therefore work in less physically tasking environment of electrical, occasionally drawing from your excellent knowledge in an auto mechanic to deliver excellently in electrical. This can also be the other way round, as each could complement the other in achieving true excellence. Doing your part in every endeavor will result in personal fulfillment and lead to the achievement of greater glory.

Sometimes it becomes a big challenge for one to keep doing his part amidst demoralizing actions and conditions. The honest retiree dies waiting for his pension stolen by a corrupt politician and senior government officials. They may soon receive a political appointment and various awards.

There might be instances where you are faced with difficult unappreciative colleagues and family members, an unsupportive spouse, or a disorganized and reckless housemate that leaves things lying around the whole house. You might also have work colleagues who leave the bulk of the job for you while they are perpetual unproductive busybodies. While it is necessary to call them to order and not excuse their irresponsible attitude, you must not, in the process, fall into the same attitude with them. A

Nigerian proverb has it that those who chase evil spirits must not in the process smell like the spirits they chase. It has always proven a no-win situation to turn two wrongs into one giant right!

Keep trying new ways to set your business in motion amidst challenges. Prioritize your activities to attract opportunities. Be ahead of your game by proper and excellent preparation through skill acquisitions, personal development, and taking the initiative promptly. Only then shall we strike our artesian well of true progress.

POSTSCRIPT

NOW SHALL WE BEGIN?

He who looks outside, dreams
He who looks inside, awakes
-Carl Jung

After the race, you consider miles covered. I'll like to think it's been an interesting and fascinating voyage. My grandfather once said that the man crushed by the train perhaps might have died of deafness. Good advice or suggestion works when the person it is offered to runs it up the flag pole.

Accordingly, Galileo Galilei, reinforcing the need to make use of knowledge, submitted, "I do not feel obliged to believe that the same God who has endowed us with sense, reason, and intellect has intended us to forgo their use."

The future belongs to the bold, the brave, those who dare to be daring! By the consequence of its ordeal, that which defies solution compels men to conceive and generate its solution as a response to meet human needs. Give the determined child a head-start, and he will leverage on it and figure out the entire complex voyage.

Reading this book has activated the mental infrastructure. All that is needed to rise is a little head-start, and you will figure the entire complex voyage. The knowledge presented in this book provides that head start!

Life in the womb is as important to existence as life outside the womb, for both are like the two sides of the same coin. This is to say that reading this book is as important as what happens after reading it.

Now that you've gotten here, this is not the end. The journey has just begun. The voyage map is spread on your lap; you can resolve to reach your heights and unleash the entrepreneur within you. I hope you have enough steam to keep you riding until you actualize your dream.

Today may be the beginning of the rest of a great life ahead. I encourage you to give what you have read the necessary push that will accelerate success. Only then will it ignite steam to power your aspirations.

Do not be afraid to dare even to err in the process. But as in an alarm which sometimes errs on the side of caution, you may only err on the side of decisiveness. In doing this, you are being conscious enough to make critical decisions and be bold enough to get prepared while working on your ideas. Of course, as always, your opportunities would come sooner because you have instigated it.

ACKNOWLEDGEMENT

This book is a product of personal experience that led to extensive research work and interviews. It is also a result of ideas and discussions gleaned from interactions with friends, clients, associates, entrepreneurs, academicians, professionals colleagues, and everyday people in the streets and authorities from various fields and endeavors. I will be constrained by time and space to mention all these beautiful minds.

To various authors, publishers, and writers whose work I quoted or used but whom I was unable to acknowledge because the sources were inadvertently lost over the period within which this book took form, and those who were quoted and acknowledged, I say a big thank you to you all.

To my dear wife, Kelechi Clementina, who has perfected the art of bringing a healthy balance to career and domestic demand, you remain my source of strength and balance. Thank you again for eliminating distractions from the home front as this book took form and shape.

Our Children Chizitere (Chizzy), Tonna, and Jidechi, thanks for your understanding and great sacrifice over the period as this dream developed while consuming much of our family time. Love you loads.

To my former lecturers who have remained friends many years after leaving their lecture halls and classes, I thank you. You inspired me in no small way both in and outside the classroom as I journeyed through life.

To a friend, mentor, boss, Professor Luke Onuoha, Author, former Vice President of Financial Affairs Babcock University and current Vice-Chancellor(Academics), Adeleke University. Deboss! This book is an inspiration from your desk years ago.

To my friends and buddies, Dr. Nwokocha Chibueze, Okeoghene Okan-gbenedio; my respect to you guys, and all my friends from Babcock University, you guys are awesome!

I am also delighted by the experiences, lessons, advice, and relentless nudge generated from my friends and clients at Savux

Solutions Ltd. This influence eventually led to the release of this book.

I am immensely thankful to Professor C. Omeonu, Vice-Chancellor Clifford University, from who I draw inspiration to keep going on my dreams consistently one step at a time. Thanks, Prof, for always being there.

My gratitude to a good friend Paul Sawa, for our brief discussion while I was toying with the idea of writing years back and scribbling things here and there. Paul immediately sent some materials and told me to take a look. I had no choice but to get committed to the early task of writing.

To my guys at Hydra Engineering, Kelechi David Okoroji -Man kele, the book might have started from a gift of writing jotter you handed me when my fiancée (now wife) threw a surprise birthday party for me at Hotoro.

Many thanks to a good friend and former colleague -Hon Kingsley Nze. Kingsley could be a writer's best friend and arguments combined. I must confess that I was pleasantly perplexed in his critique of my manuscript. He arrived at the nick of time to instigate great discussion through his deep, analytical, and critical reasoning, discussions that steered and tasked my thoughts, triggered rewriting, and improved content.

I cannot forget my father-in-law's inputs, Reverend (Dr) Alex Ugwu, who arrived at the eleventh hour and made huge suggestions that brought better flow to reading.

Martha Habu loyal and steadfast friend whose intelligence often inspires and awakens zeal to go the extra mile, thanks for always being there.

Mention must be made of my Parents:

My Mother, Mrs. Justinah Nwogu, your rugged belief in hope is a confirmation that the bold is unstoppable. May God rest your loving soul until that great getting up morning.

My Dad, Mr. Moses Nwogu, maintained that the strength of wisdom is measured by being resilient to the storms of life instead of forcing oneself to stand straight and be broken by life's vicissitudes. Now I have discovered that to reach the heights, one must stimulate and activate the entrepreneur from within and must strive to rise taller and stretch onward and upward again and again after every storm that comes your way.

To Adaku, Chinedu, Ebere, Onyinyechi, and Chucks, your bold belief in me both in 'rainy season and harmathan' of life is a testimony that those who must reach the heights of success are as determined as their support group.

My gratitude extends to great friends like Morrison Okeorji (Iroko) -early intervention in psychosis practitioners in the NHS England United kingdom who constantly persuaded me to put my thoughts in writings.

I remain grateful to my good friend Solomon Ahorituwere (Iron), who though faraway in United kingdom, has remained my 'go to' guy whenever I am stranded on internet or job-related software challenges, Iron is always there to guide me out of such cobwebs.

To a friend and bro from way back, Iyke Ikegwuonu Jnr. CEO, Seedgap Innovations Ltd UK, a UK based special innovation business offering enterprise growth solutions in Africa and emerging markets. Iyke is one Dude I go to anytime I need to stretch out some points with further clarity. Thanks, man.

Dr. Onyebuchi James Ileh, Henry Nwanguma, Bishop Beryl Esembe Nalowa, Dare Mathew, you've all inspired me in no small way. Your trust in me motivates and feeds my boldness to write.

My special thanks to Nnenna Nwakanma. I sent the manuscript to Nnenna at the point of publishing. Expectedly her advice and contributions gifted tremendous new ideas.

My gratitude to friends and entire members of Liberty Chapel Utako, Abuja. Time and space will limit me from mentioning these beautiful minds that remain my support group.

The Senior Pastor -Pastor Kayode Arigbede thank you very much for the supports. Dibugwu Udo Godwin, Nkechi Onwuasonya Fred, Idowu Ebenezer, you've been friends indeed.

To my ever faithful friend Kachi Francis Nwankwo for your unalloyed friendship and super support base, thank you.

Edwin Daniel Eukhouria of ONE Campaign, thanks for 'dropping it like it's hot whenever I run ideas with you. It helps do it better.

My special thanks also go to my Boss, Mr. Tunji Aworinde CEO, Forensic Insight International Ltd. I learned so much from you within the three years I worked directly with you.

My undiluted appreciation to my ever steadfast social media friends, crews, and paparazzi with who I often engage in mental gymnastics as we agree, disagree, align, 'scatter-balance,' rebound, and more especially learn from each other in diverse issues. And to my ever faithful followers at Chris Socials – Thank you.

You guys provide enough steam and inspiration that a better world is in the offing; let's continue to do our part in our various locations across the Globe.

And to Barack Obama, whose ascendance to the seat of power as the first black President of the United States confirms my conviction that to reach the heights, your confidence should compel people to believe and buy into your radical and audacious ideas. I remain eternally grateful to you all. I am tremendously grateful to have enlisted my publishers, Emotion Press, to be part of this project, for their uncanny patience, suggestions, and prodding over the period this book gathered steam till its completion. And to my passionate editor, Ms. Faniyi, for a diligent work, I must admit I left her a job almost as huge as writing an entire book. We shall do it again sooner. Thank you.

ABOUT AUTHOR

Chris Nwogu is an Alumnus of Andrews University, Michigan USA, and Babcock University Ilisan-Remo Nigeria. He is the Managing Director of a Marketing firm in Abuja and Founder/CEO Savux Solutions Ltd, Abuja, Federal Capital Territory, Nigeria. He was the Senior Marketing Executive at Forensic Insight International Limited Abuja, and currently consultant at Forensic insight International.

He is a public speaker and writer who write out of passion on social issues and Entrepreneurship development, especially among Millennials.

Chris has many years of successful Marketing and Entrepreneurship practice. He currently lives in Abuja, Nigeria, with his family.

ABOUT THE BOOK

The book, STREET ENTREPRENEURS, is divided into four parts of 22 inspiring and highly engaging chapters strongly bent on provoking its readers to achieve their goals by instigating and guiding them to gather the uncommon boldness, and well-planned commitment. This book is a guide to ensure success as an entrepreneur, increases self-worth, and leads to achieving one's potential.

This is a book of solutions that will dare you to take action. STREET ENTREPRENEURS will not only strive to awaken your entrepreneurial instinct successfully but will energize you to confront your fears, pursue that career, skill, or business despite lost time and confidently launch yourself to that dream that has kept you restless for long. WE ALL HAVE IT IN US TO SUCCEED!